BRINGING BACK THE
Magic

A Transformational
Memoir

MARGARET T. WRIGHT

Tewillager Publishing
A division of Equatorial Group, Ltd.
Phoenix, Arizona

Copyright © 2008 by Margaret T. Wright
All rights reserved. No part of this book may be reproduced in any form, by photocopy, microfilm, xerography, recording, or any other means, or incorporated into any information retrieval system, electronic or mechanical, without the written permission by the copyright owner.

All inquiries should be addressed to:
Tewillager Publishing, a division of Equatorial Group, Ltd.
13835 N Tatum Boulevard, #9-609
Phoenix, AZ 85032
www.MaggieWright.net

Cover design and illustration "Bringing Back the Magic" Copyright © 2008 The Wright Marketing Blueprint, Inc.

Interior Design: Julia Patterson, www.writedesignaz.com
Cover Illustration: Jason Williamson
Cover Design: Julia Patterson
Photo Credit: Mary Bloom, Page 283

ISBN-13: 978-0-9821198-0-8

Printed in Canada

DEDICATION

This book is dedicated to my spiritual sister, Sonia; to my feathered partner, Merlin Tewillager; and to all of the other incredible animals who influenced my life's transformation: Sweetpea; Kyaaro; Anassas; Josie; Prince; Gwendolyn; Wart; Mr. and Mrs. Tewillager; Buffy; Tinkerbell; Beau & Maurice; Skeeter; Wee Willie Winkie; Henry; Judd; Gwen; Abraham; Nehemiah; Isaac; Mary Martha; Sam; Sara; Cindy & Mindy; Sir & Lady Thrasher; Lucy, Beau & Junior; and Ms. Bird.

ACKNOWLEDGEMENTS

Writing a book from the heart is a major undertaking, and without the encouragement and support by a few friends and colleagues, it may not have ever been completed. I am so grateful to my friend, Jerome D. Page (Jerry), who patiently read and reacted to each chapter, as it was written. My friends and animal lover colleagues, Kim Bloomer and Jeannie Thomason of www.AnimalTalkNaturally.com, so kindly agreed to serve as "consumer readers" and to give me invaluable feedback. I would like to express my special appreciation and thanks to Ardath Mayhar and Andrew Kirby, who not only gave me editorial assistance, but they also took the time to offer quality direction to help me give this book a stronger point of view. I am indebted to Julia Patterson of www.writedesignaz.com, who did the graphics, layout, and illustrations in the book. Artist Jason Williamson did an incredible job at capturing the emotion of *Bringing Back the Magic* in the front cover illustration, and I am so appreciative to Sharon McCarthy, who connected me with Jason, Andrew, and Julia, and I thank attorneys Anna Kirschner, Genny Wall and Morgen Bowers for their guidance. Finally, I thank my inner child, Monty Wright, who helped me reach inside and connect with the feelings and memories from the past.

CONTENTS

Mama Dear's garden

prologue

MY GRANDMOTHER'S GARDEN

I love animals. I have always loved animals. Sometimes I think that I get along with them better than people. They are patient and giving, and they allow me to be myself, warts and all. Circumstances of my early childhood led me to hide from life, but my closeness with animals helped me twist and turn, and work through these behavioral phobias and fears, to become a participator in life and advocate for my special little friends. This is the story that I want to tell...

My earliest memories of my alliance with animals are from my early childhood between four and six years old. Besides my doll babies, my closest friends were my albino rabbits. My best friend rabbit named Mr. Tewillager and I had a special relationship. He and his girlfriend lived in a pen outside, but my parents would let me bring them up into my bedroom to hang out. We loved to play little hide and seek games. I remember placing little paper bags in areas of the room so that they could run and hide. It was so amusing to watch them jump up in the air, twist and turn, and run in circles right around me and the room. They would look up at me with their comical little faces, which made me laugh. Then we touched noses. Sometimes I liked to wiggle my nose at them and giggle. They brought such joy to my life.

I always saw Mr. Tewillager as magical because I thought I could hear his voice. He spoke to me telepathically. I don't know what he talked to me about but I shared with him my deepest feelings and wishes. Sometimes I built little tents in my bedroom, where pillows and chairs were placed strategically apart and a sheet was thrown over them. Mr. and Mrs. Tewillager and I crawled under the sheet to hide from the rest of the world. I hugged them, and we snuggled and wiggled our noses. I giggled. That's where we shared our deepest secrets.

When I think back to my early childhood, my first thought is always of Mr. Tewillager, my magical, white rabbit companion. He represented everything that was good.

❧

Since I could not pronounce Margaret, I called myself Monty Wright. I was very active, always exploring and getting into everything. Similar to the energizer bunny that keeps on going, I was curious and into everything in my path that was not nailed down. My personality was befitting of the name Monty.

I also was a little prissy and particular about things. For example, most women appear to be obsessed with good hair. What's even more amazing to me is that this pattern appears to go deep down into the female psyche, to little girls. Right down to the early years, it was also my obsession. I remember being jealous of

 *a childhood friend who had beautiful curly, blonde hair. Mine was mousy brown and straight as a board; but I pretended that it was beautiful anyway. My grandmother, whom I called Mama Dear, would drop by with her house man chauffeur Elijah (nicknamed Lige) to take me for afternoon car rides. Of course, I made her keep the car windows closed so that the wind "did not blow my curls."*

I cannot remember how or why I gave my grandmother the nickname of Mama Dear. Nicknames are very descriptive of personality. Mama Dear was too refined to be called grandma, gramps, or granny. She was a genteel Southern lady who loved nice things and to give grand parties. She had porcelain skin, white-silver hair, and baby blue eyes. When I think of her, I think of flowers and the color of lavender.

Accordingly, I nicknamed my grandfather Papa Dear. I didn't know him very well because he was bedridden with late stages of the Alzheimer's disease. I remember visiting him every Sunday at lunch.

Mama Dear loved to spoil me, her first grandchild. I remember every Christmas of my childhood, she sent Lige over to our house to deliver laundry baskets filled with presents for my little brother Thomas, who was two years younger than I, and me. Those were the days.

On most Sundays after church we went to Mama Dear's house

for lunch. My parents dressed up Thomas and me to the hilt. I remember wearing these frilly, froo froo dresses, which I am sure were the big brand names of the time. That kind of stuff was never really important to me, but nevertheless, we had to be dressed for the occasion.

Mama Dear and Papa Dear lived in a beautiful house on a two acre lot. Mama Dear loved flowers and landscaping, so it was always like visiting Wonderland for me. The brick walkway up to the front door was lined with beautiful pink, red, and white azalea bushes. The front yard was sprinkled with magnificent oak trees and smaller bushes. But the most exciting part was her backyard, which consisted of a side yard to the right and then a private little flower garden that was located directly behind her house. The side yard consisted of a large green area, which had groupings of small bushes and flowers scattered in the open area. A narrow brick walkway led to a little path, probably four feet wide, which encircled the large green area. The path was formed by a combination of trees with thick branches and little flowering bushes, all scrunched and huddled together on each side. It felt as if I were walking in a dark, cozy tunnel. It was a place where I could go hide. No one could see me. No one could hear me. No one could find me, except for the little backyard animals... and the imaginary diva spirits.

Even though the garden behind Mama Dear's house was small, it felt like acres to me. It was made up of four main quadrants containing the most beautiful flowers, with vibrant colors of indigo, red, violet, orange, and white. Each of these flowering quadrants was lined with ivy. They were separated by a little red brick pathway that formed the symbol of a cross. Then there was a water fountain bird bath in the middle of the garden, placed at the cross intersection of the red brick path. The fountain consisted of a statue of a little girl holding a container that spout out water into the bird bath. The little girl was named Margaret, right after me. Imagine! I wasn't even yet six years old, and I already had a "statue named after me."

My favorite activity at Mama Dear's house was to play in the yard, but I wasn't usually allowed to go out there until after lunch because I couldn't mess up my dress. So we sat around on Mama Dear's side porch and talked for a while before being called for lunch. Mama Dear's house man chef Lige would finally call us for lunch. We walked into a large formal dining room with a long, antique mahogany dining room table, which was covered by an intricately laced and designed white linen table cloth. On top of the table cloth were five settings of white linen place mats and a battery of silverware, all laid out for the various meal courses.

Sunday lunches at Mama Dear's house were quite spectacular. But the desserts were even better! We were served such dishes as Charlotte russe, chocolate souffle, and vanilla ice cream with homemade, thick chocolate sauce. And like the grown ups, I got my own coffee. Of course, it was a child's version of coffee, consisting of mostly milk with just a splash of coffee. Nevertheless, I was there with the best of them, putting on conversation and sipping my very own coffee.

Then after lunch, came the fun! Once we changed clothes, the adults escorted Thomas and me outside to play. As I got older, closer to six years, I could play with less supervision. This was my

Maggie Wright with her beloved fountain.

Mama Dear in the back garden.

Garden exploration after every Sunday lunch at Mama Dear's house.

"Monty" Wright at her second birthday party at Mama Dear's home.

most special childhood memory. As quickly as I could, I dashed for the secret, cozy path between the bushes in Mama Dear's yard. My favorite place to hide was in a little indentation between some azalea bushes and under a banana shrub tree. I grabbed a few of the banana tree fruit and squeezed them in my hand. They looked to me like little white pistachio nuts, except they were soft and gave off the most beautiful banana fruit fragrance. Then I huddled there quietly between the bushes, waiting for the backyard animals to come out. Of course, my parents knew exactly where I was, but they never disturbed me.

I remember watching a sparrow couple build their nest. One flew off into the nearby bushes and picked up a short piece of stick, or pine straw, and returned to place it between the leaves of a tree branch diagonally across from me. One at a time, each bird brought a new piece of something to place in the nest space: a little bit of string; a few twigs; a few dead leaves from the previous year; a few feathers from other birds.

Then I watched the little chipmunks scoot between the bushes. One of them darted across the path and then froze under a bush a few feet from me. Then the other one came, and they made little jibber jabber squeaks at each other. They reminded me of little toy motor cars that I played with in my bedroom. Once they were wound up, they scooted across the floor and froze immediately, when the energy ran out.

When it was time to go home, my mother and I walked to Mama Dear's flower garden so that I could pick some pansies to take home. Pansies were my very favorite flower because they had such beautiful faces. They seemed like little fairy folk, and it *felt as if they were smiling and talking to me. On windy days, their little heads swayed back and forth in the breeze, as if agreeing with my pontifications. The pansies that were lucky enough to be picked were placed in little Dixie cups with water. Then they were taken home to live in my doll house, where they became make-believe children, right along with my doll babies.*

Maggie and a favorite doll baby

chapter one

THE MAGIC ENDS

Childhood in the fifties was so different from today. Back then, you had to rely on your imagination and playing skills. I always wanted to be a teacher, so in my early years (and older), I spent many days in my bedroom classroom teaching my doll babies and pansies how to read and write. They were lined up in a row and given pieces of paper and pencils. Then I pretended to grade their papers and lecture them about things.

I also loved music and dancing. I spent hours spinning in circles with a sheet over my head, singing to Rodgers and Hammerstein show tunes that were played full blast on my little Victrola music box. Of course, I didn't know the words at that age or what they really meant... but that did not matter.

Imagination was also spent in Nature. There was a vacant wooded lot beside my house where I would sometimes go to hide and observe the movement of the birds, chipmunks, and squirrels around me. On dark rainy days, I spent hours and hours sitting on the floor in our den, huddled securely between the window sill and draped material of the window curtains, so that no one could see me. I remember staring at the puddles outside. The circular motion of the raindrops falling into the puddles transformed into flowing ball dresses of beautiful fairies dancing the waltz in the puddles. Their gowns were gorgeous, with every color of the rainbow; they were having such a wonderful time!

J grew up in Wilmington, North Carolina, and my early childhood was so happy and magical... then one day, it stopped. My Mother died of colon cancer when I was six years old; she was only 34 years old. She died within four months of the discovery of the cancer.

My father and mother's doctor made the decision not to tell Mother that she had cancer and was dying. So neither she, nor my four-year-old brother Thomas and I, ever had a clue that she was dying, until the last minute. We never had time to say good bye. I'm sure she knew, but she also knew how devastated Daddy was. Not talking about it was the only way he could handle it and stay together, and so she did not force the issue. I'm sure I knew too, at least subconsciously.

I have vague recollections of her. I remember her as a beautiful, tall, dark-haired lady who was so vibrant and full of life. I remember hanging out with her in her bedroom when she was sick from the cancer. A friend had given her a Gift Tree, and my very important job was to open a new present for her every day. The tree was about three feet tall, with many little packages wrapped in lavender and pink paper with silver ribbon hanging from limbs of the tree.

I remember being spanked when Thomas and I would chase each other in the hallway. Our noise made Mother nauseated, but we didn't know; we were just children. Daddy was so torn apart; he had to carry this devastating secret deep in his heart, day after day. He had no one to tell. He had no one to talk to, except Mother's doctor, and it must have been a gnawing burden for him.

I vaguely remember when Daddy broke the news. On Wednesday morning, May 9, 1956, Thomas and I were sent to stay with our babysitter at her family farm, because I had just contracted the mumps and Mother had drifted off into a coma, and at 7 p.m. that night, she died. On the following Saturday, which was the day after Mother's funeral, Daddy picked up Thomas and me from the farm; and before going directly home, he parked the car in a parking lot of a local shopping center, so that he could talk with us.

"Children, there's something I have to tell you," said Daddy. He paused and turned in his seat to face us. "God wanted your mother to go live with him. So she's gone to live in God's house," he added with tears dripping off of his nose. He pulled out a handkerchief from his pocket, took off his glasses and wiped his eyes. "Mother's body is living in the ground. But her soul, her spirit, and her heart have gone to live with God. Now, she is an Angel, just as beautiful as ever." [1]

That's a lot for a six-year-old and a four-year-old child to comprehend. It was like ice water in our faces. When we left, she was sick. When we returned, she was gone…dead.

According to my father's notes about that time, Thomas did not understand what Daddy meant; I had many questions. "Does she have one of those things around her head [a halo] like I wore in the Christmas play?" I asked.

"I promise you she does. She is a beautiful Angel in the sky, helping God do things for people," responded Daddy.

When we got home, he took us up into Mother's room to show us that she was gone. Her bed was all made up, as if she had gone on an errand. The room was completely tidy; her three-foot Gift Tree was no longer there. Then our maid Carrie joined us to go to the cemetery. Mother's burial site was covered by a canvas tent and there were hundreds of colorful flower arrangements all around her grave. Thomas ran over to the grave site… kneeled down and started digging at the dirt with his hands, screaming, "Mudder! Mudder! Mudder!"

When we got home, I started crying uncontrollably and ran back into my room. Daddy tried to comfort me but it was all too devastating. I asked him to let me be alone for a little while and to bring in my two rabbits, as my animals and I had a lot to think about. Moments later, the bedroom door opened and Mr. Tewillager and his girlfriend were brought in to be with me. We sat together, huddled on the floor… with the lights off.

The reality had finally sunk in. I was never going to see my mommy again. What was I going to do? How was I going to survive without her? How was I going to carry on? I had so many questions in my head. Who was going to take care of us? Why did mommy leave me? What did I do? I want her back.

Carrie came into my room to give me some lunch. I had so many questions to ask her. She sat patiently on the floor with me and Mr. and Mrs. Tewillager. She held me for a few minutes and said, "Baby, don't you cry." After lunch that day, Carrie knocked on Daddy's door. "Mr. Wright," she said. "I'm so sorry to bother you, but Margaret has a question, which I cannot answer. Do you have a moment?"

Daddy looked up and smiled, "Yes, Carrie. What is her question?"

Carrie took a deep breath and sighed. "Mr. Wright, Margaret asked when you were going to marry again so she could have a new mommy. I didn't know how to answer a question like that."

Daddy looked down and wiped a tear from his eyes with the soiled handkerchief in one of his trembling hands. He stared into space for a moment and looked back at Carrie. "Tell her that I'll think about it."

Later that afternoon, I went downstairs to join Daddy. Mother's Day was the next day. "Daddy, what are we going to give Mother for Mother's Day?" I asked.

"What do you want to give to her?" Daddy answered in a trembling voice.

"Flowers," I said.

"What kind?"

"Pansies." So Daddy ordered some pansies to be delivered to Mother's grave.

I tried hard to sleep that night, but the deep depression kept waking me up. I cried for my mommy. Please come back! The next morning, on Mother's Day, Thomas and I went into Daddy's room to wake him up. Daddy's eyes were red and wet; all three of us were so sad. "Daddy, I don't want you to marry anyone else," I said. "We couldn't find anyone as sweet and pretty as Mother." Daddy hugged me and trembled.

Later that morning, we went back to the cemetery to visit Mother for Mother's Day. Thomas and I placed our flowers by her grave, and mine were the pansies. Thomas and I had more and more questions. Daddy tried to help us understand that Mother's body was there but her heart and soul were living with God to do good things for the world. She was a beautiful angel, just like she had been on earth. The more questions Daddy got from us, the more unraveled he became. He squatted beside us by Mother's grave, and he kept looking at the ground. His eyes were full of tears and sadness; his nose and glasses were dripping from the tears; he choked and wept, and could no longer speak. Carrie noticed that he was about to break down, and so she guided Thomas and me back to the car. Daddy stayed for a few more minutes to regain his composure and to have personal words with Mother's soul... on Mother's Day.

*W*eeks later, in late June or early July, there was a heat wave in the area. The temperature had skyrocketed to August levels in the high nineties. The air was thick and listless, and it was hard to breathe.

Mr. and Mrs. Tewillager lived in a pen located under a shady oak tree in the backyard. On extreme heat and humid days, they were given relief by the mist from a revolving backyard sprinkler that was turned on every day; but for some reason on this afternoon, someone had forgotten to turn on the sprinkler.

Thomas and I returned with Daddy from an errand, and as we drove into the carport, we noticed two white carcasses lying motionless on the ground. No! Not my best friends too! I jumped out of the car screaming as I ran over to my bunnies' bodies. They were stiff as a board. I hugged Mr. Tewillager. There was no voice coming from his body; there was no life. I held him and Mrs. Tewillager and curled into a ball on the ground. Clutching them to my breast, I closed my eyes and sobbed hysterically.

Maggie's Fourth-Grade Class Picture

chapter two

GOING PHOBIC

How does one describe what it was like being a six-year-old child who had just lost her mother? Beyond fear, beyond grief, it felt as if a dark shroud of gloom had been wrapped around me. My head was filled with constant chatter. Why? What did I do? Please come back! Don't leave me, Mommy! Please come back! There was a constant aching in my heart that longed for her. No matter how beautiful the days were or how exciting it was to get new toys, nothing could make the feeling of deep and dark depression go away.

My father was devastated by this loss, for Mother was the love of his life. Daddy seemed so fragile. His beautiful blue eyes were always watery, and I could feel his grief. We stopped talking about her because it was too painful. We even stopped talking about feelings. Instead, I tried to be a stoic little soldier, just like my daddy. We were shells on the outside; but on the inside, I felt more like an abandoned and helpless baby chick that had just lost its parents to a predator, or to a car that had killed them.

Mother had been the glue of the family. How would we carry on without her? The house felt empty and dark. Day after day, I curled up on my bed and sobbed helplessly. In periods between crying bouts, I sat frozen: motionless... staring into space... hugging myself.

Not only had I lost my mother, but I also lost that magical connection with Nature. I stopped hiding outside in the woods, and I could no longer see the fairies in the water puddles. Although I still loved pansies, they seemed to stop talking to me. Playing in my grandmother's garden became ordinary. I still went to my secret places in Mama Dear's backyard, but instead, I hid to cry.

Psychologically, six-year-old children tend to believe they are very powerful because they are the center of their own world. Little girls at that age also tend to be "daddy's little girls" with platonic crushes on their fathers, and I was one of them. I had been planning to marry my daddy when I grew up. On top of that, I had had an illness at the same time as my mother had the cancer, and I had been feeling a little competitive with her for attention because I was also sick in bed, but for a shorter period. I had also been jealous of her because she could sit outside in the yard and I could not, when I was ill. Therefore, I felt guilt... that I had lived and she did not... that I ended up with Daddy and she did not.

My illness was called nephritis, which is caused by the nitrogenous wastes backing up in the kidneys, thereby making one quite sick. I have no idea how I got it. Perhaps it was because I didn't like to drink water; my parents and Carrie had to disguise it by adding food coloring to it, in order to make me drink it. Or it may also have been because I subconsciously identified with Mother, since I contracted it immediately after she got sick. I remember the day when I first woke up with nephritis: every muscle in my body ached. I was so weak that I could not get out of bed and so Daddy wrapped me up in a blanket and took me to the hospital, and a few weeks later, he brought me home. I was completely bedridden at home for a few more weeks, and I was not even allowed to get out of the bed on my own. For example, when I had to go to the bathroom or to take a bath, someone had to carry me. Once I was over the illness, I was only allowed to get out of the bed for short periods, such as for only a half hour at a time and then building up each day, until my body strength had returned. Thankfully, my health did return to normal a few months before Mother died, except for the mumps that I had contracted just before she died.

Although I was emotionally flattened by my mother's death, there was an inner strength that made me go on. I knew I had to take on a little mommy role for my brother and a stiff upper lip for my father. Someone had to carry on, and it had to be me. I had to be the strong one for all three of us. This inner strength came from my deep connection with and belief in God. Even as a young child, I always knew there was a higher power looking after me. Mother had always talked to me about how loving God was and how he assigned his angels to help people when they needed it. Every Sunday, she and Daddy took me to Sunday school and every night, we said our prayers together, so I felt very close to God as a young child. I remember over the years after Mother had died going with Daddy and Thomas to services at our church, St. James Episcopal Church in downtown Wilmington; I stood there, right beside my father, being as stoic and as strong as I could be.

When I was nine years old, Daddy took Thomas and me to talk to Santa Claus when he came to Wilmington. There was a long line of children waiting for their turns to see Santa. Each child would sit on his knee while reciting their wish lists. Then he gave them one piece of candy from a two-foot bucket and sent them on. Finally, it was my turn.

"Ho, ho, ho!" he said. "Young lady, what do you want for Christmas?"

"I want a Bible," I said.

"A Bible? How old are you?" he asked.

"I just turned nine," I answered.

"I've never had a request like that from a nine-year-old girl," he said. "Here. Take all of this. You deserve it!" Santa Claus gave me the entire two-foot bucket of candy. His helper replaced it with another bucket.

Next, it was Thomas' turn. "Young man, what do you want for Christmas?" he asked.

"I want a Bible," answered Thomas.

"That's nice, young man," laughed Santa as he gave him one piece of candy and patted him on the shoulder.

That Christmas, I got my very own Bible. It was bright red, and it had my name imprinted on the front: Margaret Taylor Wright. I spent many nights reading and trying to understand the scriptures before going to bed. I kept very quiet about my spiritual feelings over the years, as they were a part of my inner world that I did not share.

⸙

Not long after Mother's death, Daddy hired nannies to take care of Thomas and me. The first one called herself Woody. She was from England, and she had a wonderful imagination. She gave us pictures of Princess Anne and Prince Charles of England, because they were about our age. I remember pasting the postcard pictures on the walls of my bedroom and wondering what they ate for breakfast and what they did for fun. Woody came up with exciting imaginary stories about the daily activities of Prince Charles and Princess Anne. Then she gave us more pictures of the Queen's home in England, as well as more pictures of the Prince and Princess playing in England.

Our home in Wilmington was not very far from the beach, since we lived in southeastern North Carolina; therefore, Woody took us on all-day trips to the beach. It took forever to prepare: we had to pack cold drinks; sandwiches; blankets; umbrellas; little buckets and shovels for digging sand; balls for throwing; and so on. And Woody had to carry it all. She chose a different beach and a different sand dune for each occasion: sometimes we went to Wrightsville Beach, and sometimes we went to Topsail Beach, and on and on.

Then one day Woody decided that we were going to have a picnic in our backyard, instead of the beach. She tied old sheets to the trees to make a magical canopy, and then she tied balloons to the tree branches. "Margaret, here's some paper and a pencil," she said. "I heard if you write a note to the elves, they'll come into the yard to play. And they'll write us back! Let's try it!"

My heart jumped! My eyes lit up! "Wow!" I thought. "Will they come back? Will there be magic again?" This was my first day of joy! I snuck outside very early the next morning. Yes! They did write back!

A few months later, Woody resigned, and Thomas and I were abandoned again by another mommy figure. We went through five more nannies over a four-year period, none of whom were as exciting or as magical as Woody. Like Woody, many of the nannies were from Europe, and they didn't seem to remain with us any longer than approximately six months. I have no idea why they left so often, as Thomas and I got along with most of them; perhaps life in Wilmington was too quaint. One nanny, whom I did not like, was originally from Wilmington; but she had such a shrill voice that she got on my nerves. I can still remember that voice saying, "Margaret, Margaret, go to bed! Go to bed right now!" She did not stay for very long either; but that may have been because I complained about her to Daddy.

I had a lazy eye that wandered, and so Daddy took me to an optometrist who gave me glasses; but then my father took me to an eye specialist in New York City, who later took them off, stating that I would grow out of it. The coolest thing about the whole experience of visiting the specialist was that Daddy had to take me (sometimes both Thomas and me) to New York City every year for an eye check-up. I could not wait for those trips; but it was like waiting for Christmas in July, because the days leading up to our departure seemed to move slower and slower.

Not only that, we always visited the infamous toy store in the city called FAO Schwartz, so that I could get a new "Tiny Tears," which was my absolute favorite doll baby because it cried real tears and wet its pants. Like many little girl baby boomers in the 50s and early 60s, I felt like a real mommy when I hugged my Tiny Tears, because she felt so real to me. Taking care of my dolls satisfied my nurturing side; and I loved to pretend that I was teaching them because I just knew that I was going to be a teacher when I grew up.

At that time, Wilmington served as the headquarters for the Atlantic Coastline Railroad, and so we had really good rail service from Wilmington to New York City. Accordingly, we boarded the train in the afternoon and then rolled into the city early that next morning. I can remember the movement and the old material smells from being in a tiny, private sleeping car, which was only large enough for a window seat that turned into a bed and a tiny little bathroom. Daddy took the top bunk that opened out from the wall above the window seat, and I slept in the window seat bed. When the beds were pulled out, there was not much room left for moving around. I was always much too excited to sleep anyway, as I kept waking up to peek out of the window, when the train stopped at different stations on the way to New York.

Once we got to the city, we usually went straight to the St. Regis Hotel, which was located on 55th Street between Madison and Fifth Avenues; but sometimes, we stayed at the Waldorf. The book, *Eloise at the Plaza*, had just been published around that time in the 50s by Simon and Schuster, and I felt just like Eloise, who was a six-year-old child that had many adventures while living in the Plaza Hotel. I loved to race up and down the hallways and play hide and seek with Thomas, when he joined us; but of course, Daddy put a stop to it, as quickly as he could. After my doctor's appointment, we walked around the city and then went to Schwartz to find my new doll baby. At night, Daddy took me to fancy restaurants with white table cloths, where I had to be on my best behavior, and sometimes, he took me to Broadway musicals, such as the *Pajama Game* and *My Fair Lady*. Then on the next day, we took the train back home.

My yearly adventures to New York City, in addition to helping Woody write to the elves in our backyard, stand out as the experiences of my childhood that brought such joy to my heart, so much that they gave me brief intermissions from the sadness and pain caused from losing my mother. Little did I realize at the time that I would not only be visiting, but I would also be living in New York City, in my future adult life.

~◦◦◦◦~

*D*addy bought me more rabbits. I loved them and played with them, but they were not Mr. Tewillager; they did not talk to me like Mr. Tewillager. Someone had forgotten to spay and neuter one couple, and we ended up with so many babies that Daddy had to give them all away.

Then Daddy bought me a dog. He was a buff-colored Cocker Spaniel, and I named him Buffy. There had been other dogs in our family, but Buffy was the first to be my very own. Buffy lived in the laundry room and it was my job, with supervision, to feed him. We went everywhere together. He was a sweet dog, able to pick up on when I was sad. Then he would run up to me and lick my face all over, making me giggle again. He loved to play with a favorite red ball, about the size of a baseball, which he loved to fetch... and chew... and maul. It didn't last very long.

In the 50s, there were no leash laws, nor were there invisible fences, so dogs could roam wherever; therefore, Buffy sometimes followed me when I rode my bicycle to school. Then he returned home later in the morning; but one morning, he did not return because he was hit by a car while crossing the street. The witnesses to the accident told me that he kept trying to get up to keep walking. My Buffy was trying to come home to me; it broke my heart, again.

Buffy had a spirit about him that was effervescent. When I think of him, I see him prancing up to me with his tail straight up and wagging at light speed.

～ᴄᴄᏋᴄᴄ～

*W*hen I was in the third grade, Daddy sent me to camp, but I did not want to go. It was the first time I had been separated from home since my mother's death, and I did not want to be separated from my father. What if he died, just like my mother? What if he had just disappeared when I returned? I did not want to go to camp.

We stayed at the Eceola Lodge in Linville, North Carolina, on the night before being deposited at Camp Gay Valley. Daddy bought me a little doll that was made from socks. A few hours after arriving at camp the next day, I tripped on a large tree root that protruded from the ground, and it knocked all of the breath out of me. That was an omen: Camp Gay Valley did not become happy and gay for me.

I cried every night, huddled under the covers of my bunk bed, quietly sobbing so no one would hear me. I lay there, clutching that new doll, thinking about my Daddy. I lay awake in the darkness for hours, feeling my breath and listening to the melodic symphony of thousands of crickets in the woods.

～ᴄᴄᏋᴄᴄ～

*M*y second dog was a black Cocker Spaniel mutt named Tinker Bell, and she stuck by my side like glue. She was not really a game player, as Buffy had been, but she was just as loyal and loving. She was happy just lying on the grass in the yard with me, giving me comfort and support. Physical contact seemed important to her, as she always had to have a body part touching me. When we sat on the grass, she lay right beside me with her back touching either my leg or back; I think she was giving me energy.

Tinker Bell was my rock, and she was there for me every day after school. I shared with her my secrets and fears; she was the only one who would listen to me as I talked about my feelings. Whether or not she understood, she listened and accepted me, no matter what. She was my therapy dog and I do not know what I would have done without her.

I still longed for my mother and the magical wonder that I had before she died. I was drawn to wonderful books, such as *Stuart Little, Charlotte's Web*, and *Alice in Wonderland*. The animals in these books were magical… they could talk, and I longed to be able to talk with animals again. I loved the Disney movies, except they all made me cry. I was so upset for Bambi, and I understood the internal mortification that Dumbo went through when everyone laughed at him. I cried for days after watching "Old Yeller" get shot after being mauled by the wild boar.

I spent my childhood emotionally depressed. Although I carried out my day-to-day activities, such as going to school and showing up for meals, I was not completely there. I was working on half of an engine because half of my emotional energy was directed inward, in order to hold myself together.

FINDING A NEW MOTHER

As the years passed, Daddy had lots of dates, and we got lots of toys. One lady sent us two alligators from Florida; but I am sad to admit that they probably lasted two weeks, long enough to be taken to "Show and Tell" at my fourth grade class. I remember watching Daddy feed them: he had to force their food down their throats with the handle of a spoon, without getting bitten.

Finally, in the summer after I had graduated from the fifth grade, Daddy met our new stepmother. Her name was Elizabeth, but her nickname was Bobo, and so that's what we called her. We had rented a beach cottage at Wrightsville Beach, and she was staying across the street for that month. She had an imagination like Woody and played with us on the beach; and I remember swimming with her in the ocean and jumping off of her shoulders into the water. Bobo was a lot of fun, and she made my father happy for the first time in many years. After knowing her for approximately one month, he asked her to marry him; but he showed us the ring and got our permission first. Finally, I was going to have a mommy again… and perhaps I could be a child again. I decided to call her Mother.

They were married in that following October, and then they

went on a six-week honeymoon to Europe, while Thomas and I remained at home with Carrie and one of the nannies. I was so excited to have a new mother and I missed my father so much that I could not wait for them to get back. They sent us many letters and postcards, and I'm sure they called home once or twice, but I don't remember. They sent toys to both Thomas and me, but I was never able to play with mine because it had been mistakenly addressed to Thomas, instead of me. My heart was broken when Thomas received his second gift and I didn't get anything; every afternoon for almost one month, I rushed to the mailbox after school to see if I got anything... and each day, there was nothing for me. Finally, when Daddy and my new mother returned, they discovered the mistake, but it was too late because Thomas had already destroyed the toy. It was a puppet that had many strings attached for walking and moving its hands and head; but unfortunately, the strings were so tangled that they had to throw it away.

I really wanted my new mother to feel welcomed and as a part of the family, and therefore, I rarely referred to her as my stepmother. Instead, I called her Mother and referred to her as my mother; however, for purposes of this book, I will refer to her as my stepmother, so that the reader does not become confused. This childhood decision to call her Mother was not a snap judgment on my part, but I wrestled with my feelings, and since I didn't like to hurt other people's feelings, it felt from my heart like the right thing to do. Although the grief about losing my real mother was still very deep inside, as it is today, it was a way for me to attempt to move on.

My new stepmother had given Daddy a parakeet as a joke while they were dating. I have no idea why it had been a joke, except that she was terrified of birds, and they must have kidded about her fears. Of course, I loved it immediately and we named the bird "Sweetie," which I spelled "Sweatie," and I spent weeks taming him and trying to teach him to talk. Finally, he trusted me enough to get onto my hand; but when my new mother came to live with us, she gave him away, and I was forced to say good-bye. She made it very clear that there would be no more pet birds in our house. Although my connection with Sweetie was only for a short period, it was the beginning of my long relationship with pet birds, which would not be reestablished until my first African Grey parrot companion, Merlin Tewillager, entered my life in my forties.

A year after Daddy and my new stepmother married, she gave birth to my first sister and they named her Elizabeth, after my new step mom. At that time, I had just turned eleven years old and was thrilled to have a "real-live doll baby" sister to nurture. I became the live-in baby sitter and loved every minute of it. I remember helping her learn to walk; and as a result, she became the Speedy Gonzales of the Wright hallways, as she raced around the house in her walker stroller. (For those readers unaware, Speedy Gonzales was a cartoon mouse in the 1950s with the reputation for being able to run really fast.) Then I made my little sister, who was later nicknamed Lizzie, stand against the hallway walls, so that she could practice her first steps solo… no stroller. She was walking around and into everything by nine months old.

As time passed and I got older, I became more introverted and shy. My relationship with my new mother had become extremely stressful for both of us. She was only 17 years older than I, and walking into a home with two young, motherless children is difficult for anyone, much less a young woman in her middle 20s. Our difficult relationship started in that first year of her marriage to Daddy. I remember an incident in the following summer after their marriage, when we were swimming and hanging out in the ocean. I hugged her and she pushed me away, and said, "Get away! You're smothering me." I remember feeling so hurt, but then, I tried to rationalize that she may not be feeling very well because she was quite pregnant, expecting Lizzie in November, and maybe being pregnant made women overly irritable. The August weather in southeastern North Carolina was hot and humid, and getting around in a very pregnant state must have been extremely uncomfortable. But no matter how much I tried to rationalize, it really did hurt.

As I became more introverted, I spent more and more time at home eating and watching TV with Carrie. We watched "The Edge of Night" every afternoon on TV, and I drank Coca Cola and ate Oreo Cookies. There was no one to talk to about my feelings of sadness, so I shut them up by overeating. As a result, my stepmother dressed me in Chubbette Brand clothes. Can you imagine? Why would any astute marketer want to name their brand of clothing for fat adolescents "Chubbette?" It certainly did label us.

I could not understand how my new mother seemed to know when I was eating, because I made sure no one was looking when I snuck things from the refrigerator. I ate the food in a quiet corner of our den or a dark closet, without anyone seeing me. How did she know I was the one who kept nibbling at the potato salad, or eating up all of the cookies? She never saw me do it. However, it was quite obvious that it had been me, because I kept getting fatter. I remember when we rented a cottage duplex at Wrightsville Beach one summer; I snuck over to a neighbor's home to share sweet snacks. My favorite was a packaged frozen brownie dessert, which I cut it into halves, and then I would eat an entire half at one sitting. It was delicious... but not so good for me!

Not only was I fat, but I also had horrible acne that looked like boils on my face. My dermatologist gave me lots of antibiotics to attempt to clear my complexion, but it kept getting worse. In thinking back to this period of my life, while writing this book, I just want to reach back through time and hug that little girl, and tell her that everything will be alright.

LEAVING HOME

In the spring of 1963, when I was thirteen years old, my stepmother gave birth to my second sister, and she and Daddy named the baby, Eleanor, after my grandmother Mama Dear. That following fall, I was sent away to a private girls' preparatory school, and so I did not have as much of an opportunity to play with Eleanor, later nicknamed Ellie, as I had had with Lizzie. At the same time, Tinker Bell was given away because my new stepmother said the dog was too nippy to be around my young sisters. I was devastated about losing Tinker Bell, and I was upset about being sent away to school; but I was a child and did not have the power to make my own decisions about my life.

It was tradition in both my father's and stepmother's families to send the children off to boarding school; Daddy went to Woodberry Forest in Virginia and my new step mom had gone to St. Timothy's School in Maryland, when they both were teenagers. They chose St. Catherine's School in Richmond, Virginia, for me; and a few years later, Thomas was sent to Woodberry Forest. It is a big opportunity to have the good fortune to be sent to an academically strong preparatory school, as it provides one with a sound education for building a prosperous future, and many teenagers really enjoy their experiences at their prep schools. But unfortunately for me, being emotionally insecure and depressed at that time, it felt more like I was being gotten rid of, or "shipped off," as they say.

In the fall of 1963, in my ninth grade year, my parents drove me up to Richmond, and I was checked into a large dormitory bedroom with three other roommates. I was so painfully shy, and all I wanted was to find someplace to go hide, but that was no longer an option with three roommates. Instead, by day, I tried to be as polite and quiet as possible, and by night, I secretly cried myself to sleep after lights out.

Boarding school was strict, and we were only allowed a few afternoons per month to visit outside of the grounds. A few weeks after starting school, I was invited for Sunday lunch at the home of the Langdons, who were friends of my parents. I had mixed feelings about it. I couldn't wait to go to a fun luncheon, but what if I dressed wrong? What if I said the wrong thing? What if I couldn't think of anything to say? I changed my mind over and over about what to wear. Finally, the day arrived. I joined two other excited boarders in the dorm lobby. Mrs. Langdon hugged each of us at the front door and escorted us to her station wagon. Her four-year-old daughter Jeannie was sitting in the front seat, and the other two boarders and I got into the back seat. The young child looked at me. "Ick!" she said, pointing at me. "What's wrong with you? Do you have chicken pox?"

I wanted to crawl under the seat and die, as the child was reacting to my severe acne. She did nothing wrong, she was a typical, curious child; but that interaction ruined the rest of my day. I wanted to run away and cry, but instead, I sat there very politely and quietly all afternoon, crying inside.

Before going off to school, my childhood dermatologist had recommended that I undergo radiation treatment on my face, in order to cure the acne, and my parents and I had agreed. Therefore, my parents found a practitioner in Richmond, and every Friday morning for three months during that fall of my ninth grade year, I was carpooled from my boarding school to a laboratory in downtown Richmond. The practitioner led me down a hallway to a dark room; placed a metal sheet on my chest; sat behind a wall; and "fried" my face every week. It certainly was ironical because he even looked like Colonel Sanders, the fried chicken spokesman for Kentucky Fried Chicken. He was short and stubby, and he had a clump of white hair on his head and a cone-like white goatee, just like Colonel Sanders; but he wasn't as friendly. So there he was, the fried chicken man frying my face!

It turns out that the radiation treatment that was done to me and many other boomers in the 60s may have done more harm than good. Perhaps the acne growth slowed a little; but I had many basal cell carcinoma skin cancer outbreaks on my face, later in my 40s and 50s, that had to be cut off. So today, my make-up covers multiple scars on my face and nose. On top of that, because they did not cover my eyes and throat for the radiation treatments, I developed dry eye problems and had nodules on my thyroid gland in later years.

⁓∘⟨∘⟩∘⁓

*J*t was more difficult in boarding school to eat Oreo cookies, or any candy for that matter, on a regular daily basis because there were no vending machines in the dorm buildings. Instead, we were served three nourishing meals per day. The most exciting dish was called "mystery meat," which I still do not know how to describe. It was some kind of flat turkey-like meat, usually with stuffing slopped on top of it. Perhaps as a result, I did begin to lose weight.

Since I could no longer drown my sadness in food, I found another outlet: MUSIC. I had an eclectic taste, ranging from popular songs on the radio to classics by The Lettermen and Andy Williams. "Smile" was my theme song:

"Smile though your heart is aching. Smile even though it's breaking... When there are clouds in the sky, you'll get by... If you smile through your tears and sadness... You'll see the sun will come shining through for you. So just SMILE!.."[1]

I remember when the Beatles were introduced to America: it was on a Sunday night in February of 1964. All of the boarders on my floor took their spots in the television room of our dorm floor, and the black and white TV was tuned to the Ed Sullivan Show. All of a sudden the Beatles started to sing, and the teenage girls, who were standing in the television audience, started to wring their hands and cry. When the Beatles finally sang their hit song, "I Want to Hold Your Hand," the TV teens were screaming at the top of their lungs and pushing at each other to get closer to the stage. I could feel the excitement and the electricity coming through the television, and I wanted to scream too! From that night on, my new crush was Paul McCartney. I plastered posters of him all over my little section of my dorm room, and I played the Beatles music over and over and over.

I also loved rhythm and blues, which we called "beach music." It was very popular in the southeast, and it included popular 1960s R&B songs, such as "My Girl" by the Temptations; "Stay" by Maurice Williams and the Zodiacs; "Under the Boardwalk" by the Drifters; and "Be Young, Be Foolish, Be Happy" by the Tams. Beach music got its name because the R&B songs were played so often on the juke boxes at the beaches in the Carolinas and Virginia. In fact, it became so popular that a dance called the "shag" was invented to go along with it. The shag was really a version of the jitterbug, but much slower and with all kinds of fancy footwork. Many of my fellow prep school boarders practiced their shag dance steps by holding onto the doorknobs of their dormitory room doors, pretending that the doors were their dance partners.

Music played such an important role in my life because the words and the rhythm of the music allowed me to escape into the moment and unload some of my emotional heaviness. It is amazing how I may forget what I did yesterday, but the moment a 60s song plays, many of the words from that song come right back to me, just as if I had memorized them last week. For example, I remember going to a concert in our school auditorium where some of the men boarders from Episcopal High School (EHS) in Alexandria, Virginia, had come to perform for the students at St. Catherine's; and one of the young men singers smiled at me in the audience, while they were singing "Hey, Mr. Tambourine Man." He was very handsome, and I had a crush on that young man, whom I never met, for months afterwards. Now, every time I hear that song, it brings back memories of that day at the concert.

~∽∾◯∾∽~

I was seen as a loser and I had difficulty making friends at school. One night in the tenth grade, my roommates spread cookie crumbs all inside the sheet covers of my bed. To some people, this prank may be considered a funny joke to pull on a friend, but they didn't care for me, and I was not self-confident enough to be able to laugh it off. However, instead of giving them the pleasure of seeing me upset, I politely took out every cookie crumb, while laying in the dark under the sheet covers and dumped them onto the floor, pretending nothing was wrong.

As the years passed, I became shyer... afraid to talk. I was even afraid of my own shadow and terrified of standing out in any situation: I just wanted to disappear. In other words, I had lost my confidence and had turned phobic.

When I visited home in Wilmington for the weekend for my sixteenth birthday, my stepmother gave me a surprise party. She put on a luncheon at the local country club and invited ten childhood friends. We were sitting in a circle around the table; eight of the girls were talking at the same time in loud, excited voices. They were having so much fun talking about boyfriends, clothes, and movies, but mainly boyfriends, and I was too shy to talk about boys. Besides, I didn't meet many boys in boarding school. I did not open my mouth during the entire luncheon that was put on for me. I just observed and listened, wishing to be back in my bedroom at home.

I had become tongue-tied... afraid to mumble a word. In most conversations, especially with kids my age, I got nervous and forgot what I was saying the moment I felt that attention was being focused on me. I had anxiety attacks. It felt as if a motor inside my body had clicked off. I would hold my breath and almost collapse, and then I forgot what I was saying. I was hyper-ventilating, and I heard ringing in my ears. I had difficulty pulling out the right words to express things. It felt as if my brain computer had forgotten where some of my memory files were. It was frightening.

When I was uncomfortable in situations, I just learned to be physically there, but mentally gone. I sat there without saying a word...pretending to listen. I could not repeat a conversation, even if my life depended on it, because I was not listening. Instead, I was in a daydream state, where I focused on my inner world. It took enormous strength just to hold my feelings inside, because I feared exploding, with all of my doubts and anxieties tumbling onto the floor for everyone to see.

My junior and senior years in prep school were better than my freshman and sophomore years, and I had a nice roommate for both years with whom I got along. Her name was Betsy, and she was from a small town in Virginia. She had a good heart and she was not very judgmental. We enjoyed taking the bus to downtown Richmond on Saturdays to explore and then to go to the movies, as we were given a little more freedom to leave the grounds as juniors and seniors.

As they say, "rules are made to be broken," and at St. Catherine's at that time, you could be suspended from school, if you were caught smoking or drinking. Therefore, many mischievous teenage boarders started to smoke. As a matter of fact, there was a restaurant that was just a few blocks from the school, and many of the boarders went there to sneak their cigarettes. They called the restaurant "Dailies," as a code instead of its real name, and because they went there so frequently, almost daily. Betsy and I succumbed to this subversive venture, too. Especially in our senior year, when we could go off of campus during the weekday afternoons, in addition to the weekends, we snuck over to Dailies after school to sneak a cigarette or two, and then before dinner, we smothered ourselves with perfume to mask the cigarette odor. This marked the beginning of my many years of smoking cigarettes, which lasted into my forties.

I remember that feeling on the first time that I smoked. It was in a quiet corner of the Dailies restaurant; I got very dizzy, and I was glad that I had been sitting down. My excuse for continuing to smoke was that it would stop me from gaining weight; and as the years progressed, that was basically true for me. I started on Tareyton cigarettes, and a decade later, I switched to Winston Lights. Over the years, I really loved smoking, even though I knew it was bad for me. It was my crutch, and I was very hooked, both physically and psychologically.

My boarding school years had been extremely difficult for me because I was feeling displaced. In my absence from my Wilmington home, my step mom and Daddy had created their own daily routine, bringing up two precious little girls, and the attention was centered on the lives and accomplishments of my little sisters. There is nothing wrong with that. My bedroom was the same, and I was included in all family activities when I was home on special weekends, holidays, and the summertime; therefore, based on appearances, nothing had changed, except that I felt like I was not very important, a stepchild. In contrast, St. Catherine's was a great school and I was fortunate to have been accepted there; but in that time of the 60s, there were no counseling services, nor "nurturing" housemothers or teachers, to help depressed teenagers like me. Or if there were, they did not notice me. All I wanted was a nurturing mother-like figure to guide me, to let me know that someone loved me; but instead, I felt like a rudderless boat caught between two large ships that did not notice me. Therefore, I found myself muddling along, trying to grow up, as best as I could.

In looking back at my time in prep school, I now see that being thrust out on my own was actually good for me, because it left me without a private bedroom in which to hide and it forced me to begin the process of becoming my own mother. I had learned a major life lesson: only I was going to help me.

I loved to play games with the seagulls on the beach.

chapter three

LIGHT AT THE END OF THE TUNNEL

I had always dreamed of going to college at the University of North Carolina at Chapel Hill, and so my plan was to attend a two-year college in the northeast, and then to transfer to Carolina as a junior. At that time, UNC had just begun allowing a small allocation of women students to attend as freshmen, and so I figured that it would be easier to wait until my junior year, when they accepted a higher volume of women. Therefore, I attended Centenary College in New Jersey for my freshmen and sophomore years of college.

Centenary turned out to be a very positive change for me because I made friends more easily there than in high school, and I used this new situation as an opportunity to be bolder. I believe that God helps those who help themselves, and He was helping me work through my phobias and fears, through one life experience at a time. No matter how afraid I was, I faced each situation head on. When negative tapes came up in my head (You can't do this…You are a loser… No one likes you), I kept telling myself that I could do it.

I forced myself into situations that made me uncomfortable, in order to face my own fears, and slowly, I became more confident.

My two closest friends at Centenary were Alexandra and Helen. Alexandra was a beautiful, tall, young woman with large, expressive brown eyes and a big smile that lit up her face. She called herself Alex because her father had always told her jokingly that he had wished that she was a boy. My other friend Helen had long red hair. Everywhere we went, Alex's outgoing personality lit up the room, while Helen and I followed along for the fun. Alex gave me the nickname of "Mac," to coincide with her boyish nickname of Alex, and this allowed me the opportunity to break out of some of my shyness. It was kind of like acting where I was able to become a little more outgoing by pretending to be someone else. With a nickname like Mac, I was able to be lighter and to show my sense of humor. My "Southern-Belleness" was a novelty, and of course, the War between the North and South became a joke between me and my "Yankee" student colleagues.

I joined a local campus sorority and went with friends to many fun parties, and some of them were quite boisterous with beer battles. For example, the basement floor of the fraternity house at one of the men's schools was covered with beer, and the fraternity brothers competed to see who could slide further on the wet, beer-laden floor. I was extremely conservative sexually, and so this late 60s period of sexual experimentation was unnerving for me. I had crushes and dated a few young men, but nothing ever manifested into a relationship because I was seeking emotional connection, which was hard to find at that time. So I never felt comfortable enough to get involved too deeply sexually; but I did love to drink beer and party.

Karen, my freshman year roommate, was from Pennsylvania. She majored in radio and TV, and she planned to become a television producer. Karen was also voluptuous: she had shoulder-length, brown, wavy hair; an olive complexion; large oval green eyes; and a knockout figure. As a matter of fact, Karen came to visit me at Wrightsville Beach during the summer after our freshman year to attend one of my debutante parties. When she sunbathed on a raft in the ocean, the lifeguard drove by every five minutes to 'take a peek' with his field glasses. The night of the party, she wore a flowing yellow silk evening gown that displayed her cleavage. That, in addition to her glowing tan and sparkling green eyes, commanded the attention of every man in the ballroom. It was funny to watch Karen walk around in the club with a string of 10 guys following her in a straight line, panting just like little puppies. That weekend, every young single man in town knew who I was and where I lived.

Throughout my life, I had always wanted to be an elementary school teacher. Accordingly, my courses focused on early childhood development. As a part of my child psychology class, I had to observe a child for the semester and write a report on him or her. I was assigned the five-year-old son of one of my professors. Little Harry and I spent many afternoons together, playing in his yard and going to town for an ice cream cone. On Halloween night,

I was the official escort while we walked from house to house throughout the village to trick or treat.

Fun at Carolina

My wish came true, and I was accepted at the University of North Carolina at Chapel Hill for my last two years of college. There were approximately 20,000 students on campus, which was a heck of a lot more people than the few hundreds that had attended both my junior college and prep school. As a result, there were fewer rules and fewer authority figures looking over one's shoulder, and therefore, it felt as if I were completely on my own.

It was extremely difficult for students from out-of-state to attend Carolina; therefore, those who were accepted were usually incredibly smart. My junior year roommate Mary was from Delaware, and she had a double major in philosophy and religion. We spent many late-nights, until 2 or 3 a.m., discussing philosophical concepts. I wondered if our universe was one cell within a larger living body. And then I wondered if the cells in our bodies had universes of living beings within them too. Were there parallel universes? Was there another person who looked exactly like me going through similar experiences? What was reality? Are our waking lives really dreams? Are our dreams really the waking lives on other planes? How did God create all of this?

One night Mary said, "Margaret, you are really smart; but no one would know it because of the 'small' words that you use." So, I wasn't William Buckley; but I took this off-handed remark as a major compliment. No one had ever told me that I was smart. Instead, I had always been reminded by my previous life experiences and my family that I was quite the opposite. After all, I had always made average grades in prep school, and was never considered to be that smart, when compared to the rest of the high-achieving students; but I had also been burdened with depression that was holding me back from full concentration. So maybe I really was smarter than I had thought.

That fall, Mary and I were asked to play Santa and Ms. Claus for the entire dorm of 500 people for the Christmas party. Are you kidding? Me? The dormitory prefect wanted the two of us to get out there and perform in front of people? Why? Why me? No! What if I faint in front of everyone? What if I forget what I'm saying? The tension from the fear slowly built up in my body. I could feel it slowly rolling through my body, similar to that of an egg that has been cracked on one's head... the yolk slowly drips down the hair and face and along the body, right down to the feet. It was a debilitating feeling; but I believed in facing my fears, and so I decided to do it anyway. Mary wanted to be Santa, and I agreed to be Ms. Claus.

The days leading up to the performance were nerve wracking. I attempted to continue with my daily chores; but every few hours, a feeling of gloom and fear arose inside me. I stopped what I was doing and talked to myself under my breath: "I can do it. It's no big deal. It won't last very long. It's okay, Margaret, you can do it!" Finally, the fear and anxieties melted into thoughts of whatever I was doing. This process went on and on.

A few hours before our entrance, I placed my wardrobe on my bed: a red mini skirt; an extra large red sweater from a thrift shop; bunches of socks for stuffing in strategic places on my person; a small baby pillow for extra tummy padding; and of course, a pair of reading glasses. An hour later, we started dressing. First, I put on my make-up, and then, I poured white baby powder all over my hair to add a silvery cachet. I taped the baby pillow to my tummy and stuffed the socks into a D-cupped brassiere. Finally, I dressed in the red mini skirt and sweater. Mary Santa placed a regular-sized pillow on her tummy, and she wore a large pair of red pants with suspenders and a jacket. Her hair was also silver, and she also wore a long white beard. We were set.

It was time! We made our way through the audience to the front of the reception room, after strategically tip-toeing over feet, legs, and bodies.

"Ho, ho, ho! Merry Christmas!" Mary shouted. "I'm Santa and this is my sweet missus. Why Missus Claus, you DO look lovely tonight."

"Why thank you, sweetums," I replied. I shrugged my shoulders, tucked my chin into my neck, gazed at the floor and giggled shyly. Then I looked over at Mary Santa. "You look pretty good tonight, too!"

The audience laughed as they looked at our outfits and watched us pretend to flirt. A girl on the front row reached over to tug at Mary Santa's pants leg, and I swatted at her hand. "Now, now," I reprimanded. "He's MY man! Aren't you, Santa?" Mary Santa gave me this exasperated look. The audience roared with laughter. It was becoming funny and fun! Our little charade lasted about an hour, followed by a cookie and punch reception. Yes! We did it! I got through my fears. I slept well that night.

This experience was much more significant than I had realized because it gave me the confidence to step out there in front of people. I was asked to get out there and perform, instead of one of my other dorm mates, and by golly, I did it well! It was another life lesson of learning to face my fears, instead of hiding from them. I learned to stand up and work through whatever fears and anxieties that I had, and I learned that it if you face your fears with perseverance, they will eventually turn into confidences. Taking tiny baby steps, no matter how small, such as pretending to be Ms. Claus, can actually transform into life altering successes.

Another friend Bill at UNC had a cousin who had a pet Mynah bird. The Mynah is in the crow family, and it is touted to be the best talker of all of the birds, including parrots. The bird could copy the speech of his owners meticulously; and Bill loved to repeat stories that his cousin had told him about this bird. Here is an example:

His cousins, the Joneses, were away from their house. A repairman came to the door and rang the bell. The bird said, "Who's there? Hello. Who's there?"

The repairmen replied: "It's John Smith. I'm here to repair your toilet."

"Come on in. Who's there?" said the Mynah.

"I just told you. I'm John Smith, and I am here to repair your toilet," replied the repairman.

"Come on in. Hello." John Smith tried to open the door, but it was locked.

"Hello, hello. Come on in," repeated the Mynah. The repairman shook and rattled the door, and finally, he angrily walked away, never figuring out that it was a bird. The Joneses found out about this interlude because the repairman had refused to return to the house and the company had to call the Joneses to inquire what had happened.

Bill came up with story after story about the antics of this incredible creature. Every time we spoke about it, I felt a tingle of excitement, as it brought back my yearnings for my childhood days before Mother died. I jokingly told him that one day, I was going to live with a talking bird. The bird's name was going to be Merlin Tewillager Wright. That was MTW, right after my initials. "Merlin" stood for the Druid magician of Camelot. "Tewillager" was after my magical rabbit companion from childhood, Mr. Tewillager. And "Wright" was after me. It was a constant joke while I was at Carolina, and little did I know at the time that this was actually a major prediction for my future.

Summers between school years in both high school and college were spent with my family at Wrightsville Beach. It is a charming family beach, approximately 20 minutes from Wilmington, and it was named after Wrightsville Sound, which had been named after my family because they had had a lot of real estate in that area. It is completely surrounded by water with the ocean on one side and the sound on the other, and it is about five miles long and one mile wide. Our family cottage was located on the south end of the beach. It was light, airy, and impeccably decorated by my new mother, with three bedrooms on the main floor and three more bedrooms on the ground floor. It was my most favorite place to be because I felt so relaxed and free at the beach, which must have been due to the wonderful ions coming from the ocean that was right in front of our cottage.

My most favorite memories are of walking on the beach, where the seagulls and I played games with each other. I walked slowly, step by step, behind a seagull that was looking for a scrap of food left from a picnic. He stopped; I stopped, and then, we both turned around. I walked away while the bird cautiously followed me for a few yards. Then he stopped, and I stopped. We gazed at each other. I giggled. Sometimes we continued the game, and sometimes I just kept walking.

The summer between my junior and senior years at Carolina was when I met my first love, and his name was Charlie. He was six feet tall, with white blonde hair that just barely covered his ears and crinkly brown eyes that sparkled when he smiled. Charlie had enlisted in the army and was stationed at Ft. Bragg; but his parents lived in Wilmington. They were close friends with the parents of my good friend Ruthie, who also lived in Wilmington. Charlie came home every weekend because Ft. Bragg was only a few hours from Wilmington. One Saturday, I was over at Ruthie's house when Charlie dropped by to deliver something for his mom, and there was an instant attraction.

As the summer progressed, Ruthie started dating Charlie's cousin, Stuart. The four of us did everything together every weekend when Charlie came home. Charlie's parents had a small vacation house on the Intracoastal Waterway, about 30 minutes north of Wilmington, and every Saturday and Sunday, we drove up there to spend the day. We packed beer and fishing rods in Charlie's motorboat, and then we drove the boat out into the Atlantic Ocean to troll for bluefish or mackerel, and in the evenings, we feasted on our catch of the day.

I loved to observe nature around the house. I remember watching a Salt-water Marsh-hen teach her young babies survival skills. There were four chicks: three were brown in color, just like mother hen, and the fourth one, who fol-lowed up the rear, was black. Mother hen methodically walked through the marsh grass, which almost a foot tall, flattening down parts to make a trail for her babies to follow. She stuck her beak into a fiddler crab hole and then kept walking. The baby chicks followed in single file. One at a time, each chick stopped at the fiddler crab hole to stick in its beak. Each of the three chicks followed mother right through the trail, but the different-colored one had a mind of his own. After sticking his beak into the hole, he turned to the left to blaze a new trail through the marsh grass, but he could not get through. Then he turned to the right to blaze another trail, but the tall grass did not give way there, either. Finally, he fell backwards onto his butt, stood up, and then headed straight down the path that his mother had blazed.

My heart melted as I watched this fourth little chick, because he reminded me of myself. I had a self-image of being like a weed that, no matter how many times it was uprooted, it always came back. Each time it came back, it was stronger. So together, this little chick and I blazed our own trails and experiences, and I wished for a happy ending for both of us.

Then unfortunately, Charlie was given an assignment to be stationed in Germany; he had to leave in the early fall. We communicated by mail and occasional telephone calls, and our initial plan was for me to visit him in Germany in that following summer. As the months passed and the time got closer to the planned trip, I got cold feet. Although I really loved him, I realized that I was not mature enough to make such a big commitment and to travel alone to a foreign country. He was hurt and broke off our relationship; and I was devastated.

FOLLOWING MY DREAM

After college, I realized my childhood dream. In 1972, I returned to live in Wilmington in order to teach school… the fourth grade. I was not a typical teacher. I taught students the correct curriculum, as every teacher did, but sometimes in a less conventional way.

For example, it was Halloween day, and the students were going to lunch and recess. As they left, a teacher friend, who was all dressed up as a rag doll to celebrate Halloween, dropped by to chat. We decided that, in the Halloween spirit, the last period of the day should be creative and fun. The plan was to move a few things around in the classroom and then to make the kids guess who did it, and then to write about it. So my teacher friend, Elizabeth, moved around some of the students' desks, and we went to lunch, giggling.

"Miss Wright! Miss Wright!" called fourth grader Buddy, running into the cafeteria. "Miss Wright, someone has been in our classroom and messed it up!"

I looked up. "Oh no, Buddy!" I said. "Who could have done something like that!?!"

"I think you did it, Miss Wright," he answered.

"Oh, no! It wasn't me! Why would I do something silly like that?" I said with tongue-in-cheek. After all, my friend Elizabeth had done it.

A few minutes later after recess, I joined the students in the classroom. "Class," I said. "Someone has been in our classroom and messed it all up. Let's write a story about who did it. Please take out your paper and pencils and write a short story about it. Then take out your crayons and make a drawing about your story." Twenty to thirty minutes later, as I was preparing to get each student to stand up and read their story to the class, there was a knock on the door. "Miss Wright, I'm sorry to bother you," said a tall lady at the door. She was impeccably dressed, with every hair in place. "My name is Emma Tomes. I'm from the Department of Education, and I'm here to evaluate first year teachers. Do you mind if I join your class for the rest of the afternoon?"

"You are certainly welcome," I answered. "Class, this is Ms. Tomes. She wants to hear your stories." I explained that it was creative writing time and that the students were writing short stories about whom they thought had come into the classroom earlier in the day to mess it up.

I sat in a chair in the front of the classroom; the students came to the front of the room and stood beside me to read his or her story and show their drawings. I liked to be there for moral support for the students who were shy, as I had been at their age. Twenty minutes later, after about half of the class had read their stories, the door flew open. My teacher friend Elizabeth, still wearing the rag doll clothes, rushed into the classroom and slid on her feet, "Miss Wright!" she sang.

Normally, I would have jumped up to do a silly slide too, while chiming, "Ms. Berman!" But on this day, I had this impeccably dressed evaluator observing me from across the room. So this time, I looked over in a ladylike manner and smiled. "Hello, Ms. Berman. How are you this afternoon?" Elizabeth looked at me and then she saw Ms. Tomes.

"Oops," she said. "I'll see you later!"

Once the door was closed, we continued with the rest of the students reading their stories and showing their drawings. At the end of the day, Ms. Tomes came up to me. She said that she was extremely impressed, and I wanted to faint. I slept well that night, too!

❧

While I was living in Wilmington, some Republican Party officials approached me about working on the campaign to elect Jim Holshouser, who was a moderate Republican, to be the Governor of North Carolina. They approached me because I had been briefly involved with some student political activity while at UNC. There had not been a Republican governor of North Carolina in 72 years, and so I agreed to help out, because I liked the idea of having a two party system in the state. Therefore, in addition to teaching school, I became the Youth Coordinator for New Hanover County, the county seat for Wilmington, and I worked with Isabelle the County Coordinator and the team that she had pulled together to build awareness for Jim Holshouser.

This was an incredible opportunity for me because it helped to build self-confidence, and it re-introduced me to Wilmington. I was no longer seen as Tom Wright's shy daughter, but I became accepted as a competent young adult. I assisted Isabelle in organizing door-to-door campaigns and multiple rallies and fundraisers for Jim. To me, it felt like the equivalent of organizing cocktail parties, which, while growing up,

I had observed my step mom doing quite beautifully. It was another lesson that I had learned: find something that you can be good at and focus on it. I had found that I was good at interacting with people and organizing functions, especially when they were social and lots of fun.

Well, guess what! We won! After his inauguration, Governor Holshouser recommended me for a job with a new agency that had just been created by the NC General Assembly, which was named the Governor's Advocacy Council for Children and Youth (child advocacy). I decided to take the job in Raleigh, North Carolina, because I felt that it was a chance of a lifetime and I could help many more children with this job than through teaching.

I was terrified about the new job; and it felt as if all of my insecurities were coming back. What if I can't do it? What if I say the wrong thing? When I get nervous about something, I tend to get spaced out and flustered, and this time was no different. The day before starting my new job, I went to a local Raleigh shopping center to find some toiletries, and all of a sudden, without looking, I walked right into a sign that was in front of a store and cut my forehead. Therefore, on my first day of work, I walked into my new office with a big gash and bruise on my forehead. What an exciting way to start a new job!

My first project was to create a statewide hotline system. If anyone had any problems dealing with children's issues throughout North Carolina, they were to call me... shy me... and I would cut the red tape for them. I remember when I got my first calls. I did not have a clue what to do. I sat there, sometimes for entire afternoons, wondering what to do. Sometimes, it took hours just to build up my courage and to craft the appropriate words in my head, before making one phone call. I wanted to hide in a cave. Why was a tough job like this, one where I had to be bold, being given to me? What was God doing to me?

Somehow, I made the telephone calls and resolved issues for people and their children. I was developing a track record. Some of the cases were easy, while others were very complicated. In some cases, I helped people get their children into special education programs; in others, I served as a referral system. I remember being called to help a man in an extradition case because his wife had kidnapped their children. With each case, I had to study the issue and identify potential solutions… and then negotiate with the agencies for the callers.

The hotline had become so successful that I was instructed to create a public relations campaign for it. Not only that, I had to go out and publicize it myself. I dutifully contacted the top newspapers across North Carolina and traveled to the cities to interview with the reporters. It was nerve-wracking. I remember finishing my interview with a reporter in one of the cities: I walked her to the door; looked her straight in the eye; and then gave her a firm handshake. "You are a good politician," she said.

I stepped back in shock. "What do you mean?" I asked.

"You shook my hand," she answered. "That's what a savvy politician does."

"Oh no," I answered. "I shook your hand because I'm a lady FIRST and then a politician." Then we smiled and she left.

I returned to the office. The article was published in the Sunday Times of that city, and it turned out to be the most comprehensive and positive article that I had ever read about the concept of child advocacy and what we were doing for children throughout North Carolina. Not only that, it was a full-page cover story on one of the home sections of the Sunday paper. I called the reporter and thanked her, and I slept well that night!

⟨◦⟩

*I*n total, I had interviewed with approximately 30 newspapers throughout the state. Then I was asked to give speeches. Oh my God! How was I going to handle this? Talking to a reporter one-on-one was scary enough; but now, I had to stand in front of groups of people? Was I going to pass out? Was I going to have an anxiety attack? Was I going to just die, right there in front of them? What if I forgot what I was saying? What if I got so nervous that I couldn't talk?

One of my first invitations was to speak at the Bowman Gray School of Medicine "Grand Rounds." That meant intelligent doctors and interns; "Grand Rounds" sounded so ominous. You've got to be kidding! Not me! No way! Thinking about it made me shiver. I had a fearful image of being a small prey animal on the stage floor of a humongous auditorium, and a giant floodlight was shining right down on me. It was filled with people looking down at me and screaming. This was a waking image...not even a dream! How was I going to handle this one? So I kept telling them I was busy. Finally, one of the senior professors threatened to go over my head to make me find the time, and so I finally agreed.

Weeks before this meeting, I felt nervous anxiety. No matter what I was doing, there was sadness and fear in my gut. I tried to stay extremely busy so I wouldn't have to think about it, but the fear kept creeping up; sometimes I was so anxious that I felt as if I wasn't even in my body. I practiced my talk over and over and over, but it didn't help my fears. What if they asked me a question that I could not answer? What if I looked stupid? What if I passed out in front of them? What if I froze and forgot what I was saying? What if I had a heart attack and died, right in front of them?

I had only given a few talks this far in my life, and I got through them very well; but that didn't seem to help me eel better. It felt as if I had never been on stage before. The anxiety for speech number ten felt as deep as it did for speech number one. Where was this insecurity coming from? Why was I so troubled? There were people who loved to give talks; why wasn't I one of them? Why did I choose a job that made me deal with this? Why couldn't I just go into my little corner and be left alone? Why was God forcing me to do this?

Finally, presentation day arrived; I went to the Bowman Gray School early and was guided to the auditorium. It wasn't as big as I had imagined, and the lighting wasn't as bright as I had imagined, either. I remember being so tired because I got very little sleep the night before. An hour later, the doors opened and streams of young, attractive men and a few women strolled into the auditorium. There must have been 50 students sitting in different parts of the auditorium. I took a deep breath and gave my talk. The speech went smoothly and I answered all of the questions. It was another success under my belt. I slept really well that night!

Soon enough, I had handled over 100 hotline cases. Then I started analyzing the calls to determine any trends; many of the cases related to children who did not fit into the existing services. There were programs to help mentally retarded children, and there were also programs to help emotionally disturbed children; but the children that were being brought to my attention had both problems. They were both mildly retarded and emotionally disturbed, but there were no programs that met both of these needs. As a result of this analysis, I started talking up this problem with other agencies.

∽

In 1974, our child advocacy agency was restructured along with two other agencies, to form the North Carolina Office for Children. Its mission was to conduct monitoring, planning, and advocacy services for children throughout North Carolina. Along with another just being formed in Massachusetts, these were the first of their kind; we were pioneers in the field of child advocacy.

I was named Region Director, in charge of one fourth of the state.

Here I was: a shy woman of 25 years, now the youngest and only female Region Director for Human Resources in my particular region. Oh my God! How did I get there? The other Region Directors in my region were older men in their 50s and 60s. My office was located in Winston-Salem, North Carolina, and my region covered the central Piedmont area. It included cities such as Greensboro, Winston-Salem, and High Point, in addition to more rural areas. Four wonderfully competent people reported to me. They lived in different cities in my region, and they interfaced with the local community agencies, such as mental health, public health, social services, and the school systems. Our job was to identify issues, problems, and gaps in services for children, and to work with the agencies to resolve them. We also worked with volunteer groups, such as the Junior League, to create local advocacy groups within their communities.

Six months into the job, one of my staff and I attended a regional Mental Health meeting. This was a normal bi-monthly meeting where mental health professionals met to discuss particular children's cases and to come up with solutions for helping these specific children. The room was crowded with approximately 75 people. One of the many cases was that of an adolescent who was mildly retarded and emotionally disturbed, and he needed placement in a program. I was very familiar with this problem, since I had been talking up the issue of the lack of programs for mildly retarded and emotionally disturbed children. I was also familiar with this young man's case because it had been discussed and placed on hold for several months. On that day, there was another motion to postpone the case; that child's life was hanging.

"No one is leaving this room until this child's fate is determined," said a voice.

"Who said that?" I thought. "It wasn't me. Oh my God, it WAS me!" I was standing up amid this crowd of mental health professionals, telling them they could not leave the room. What had I done? There was not a sound in the room, except for the "whirring" noise from the air conditioner. "Excuse me," asked the meeting chairperson. "What did you say?"

"I said that no one is leaving this room until something is done for that child. His life has been hanging for months."

As I looked around the room, I saw faces and ALL eyes were focused on me in disbelief. The chairperson quickly recruited a small group of people to meet the next day to develop a plan for the child. It was done.

The entire mental health system across the state of North Carolina was in an uproar about my behavior. There were petitions to the NC Secretary of Human Resources to fire me on the spot. How could anyone be so bold as to stand up like that? No one would talk to me, but Secretary Johnson had a twinkle in his eye because I was doing my job. I was being a child advocate. Bravo.

In his wisdom, Secretary Johnson assigned me the task of writing a position paper about a Right to Treatment lawsuit that was being brought against the State of North Carolina at that time. I diligently studied the facts; interviewed people; and wrote my report; and it turned out that the professionals in the mental health system were impressed with it. They finally realized that I was not trying to over-power anyone, but I was acting from integrity and from my heart. They finally saw that I had been sincerely trying to help that mildly retarded and emotionally disturbed young man. Six months later, I was acknowledged and honored at a Mental Health luncheon.

We were helping thousands of children in the State of North Carolina. We worked as mediators and advocates, bringing the different departments together to coordinate and improve programs. I remember leading teams to evaluate mental hospital programs and training schools (reform schools) and making recommendations for improvement. It was an exciting time for children.

Technically, in child advocacy, I had been conducting marketing. For example, through my hotline, I had identi-fied a market need in North Carolina for a program to help children who were both mildly retarded and emotionally disturbed. I wrote a position paper about the need and distributed it throughout the child services system, and each of my staff emphasized the problem area in their respective community meetings. Then we let the issue build; it became a top priority for many child services personnel throughout the state. A program for emotionally disturbed and mildly retarded children was finally established in Raleigh, North Carolina, a few years later.

My child advocacy career was one of the most significant experiences of my life, because I was able to transform from being a terrified little girl into a powerful nurturing mother. I had learned even another lesson: when one focuses on an important cause that is "bigger" than oneself, it is easier to reach out and stand up for the cause, in spite of shyness. The many children whom I helped were actually projections of me helping myself. It was as if I were unconsciously re-righting the damage that had been done in my own childhood.

I loved living in New York City.

chapter four

NEW YORK CITY: HERE I COME!

"Look to your left. Look to your right," said a professor at business school orientation. "One of you will not be here after Christmas break." These were the first words stated in our business school orientation meeting. What had I gotten myself into?

Our Human Resources regional office had hired the Babcock Business School faculty at Wake Forest University to run a week-long communication workshop for the Region Directors and our key staff. I was really impressed with the professors who trained us, and they recommended that I apply to business school. Business school! You've got to be kidding! Am I smart enough to do that? I decided to apply because I had come to believe on the child advocacy job that I could do even more for children and the world by becoming a powerful community leader. I had been so impressed with the sharp women in the Junior League and other organizations, who had community presence and the power to get things accomplished. So I took the GMAT test, and they accepted me!

The Babcock school was young. Most of the professors had their Harvard MBAs, and that, in combination with RJR Reynolds donations, made a promising formula for a successful business school. Now, the challenge for me was to stay in.

The first year of business school was harrowing. Not only did I have to relearn how to study, but I also had to learn to give up control and follow the lead of the professors. I was a few years older than most students and had been out of the habit of studying. My social life transformed into a study group, where five of us worked together. We studied for 70 hours per week, outside of class hours. We ate together; we spent weekends together; and we kept each other in school.

The second year was much easier. That's when we started interviewing with companies. At the time, the corporate headquarters for Wachovia Bank was in Winston-Salem, not far from the Babcock School; a position at Wachovia was a cherished dream for many Babcock students. The bank executives were particular about who they hired, as their interviewing process was extensive and challenging. One other student and I were being interviewed for their bank marketing program. After taking me through the long process of talking with 27 people, they were ready to offer me a position.

The telephone rang. "Hello, Margaret," said a voice. "This is Jonathan Jason from Wachovia Bank."

"Hello Mr. Jason," I answered. "What a pleasure to hear from you!" Mr. Jason was the Senior Executive in charge of bank marketing.

"Margaret, we have a slight problem." He stopped for a moment. "We were preparing to offer you a position with Wachovia. All of my staff were highly impressed with you. So, we pulled out your original application, in order to do our paperwork before offering you a job." He stopped again. "We discovered a problem…"

A problem. My heart started pounding. I really wanted that job! After 27 interviews, they discovered a problem.

"We finally realized that you are Tom Wright's daughter. He is one of the members of our Board of Directors. We cannot hire you because of our nepotism policy."

"Oh no!" I said. "I thought you knew that all along and it wasn't a problem. I really wanted to work for Wachovia!"

"We wanted to hire you too! You are one of our favorites. You could ask your father to resign," he said.

"I don't think I could do that," I said. "He is very proud of that honor."

"We are so sorry to put you through so much and then not be able to offer a position. Actually, we are embarrassed and mortified," he said.

"This is really upsetting! I wanted to work there so badly," I answered.

"There is one thing we can do for you. We will set up

interviews for you with the top banks in any city that you request," he said. "Not only that, but we will give you a glowing recommendation."

"Thank you!" I said.

"Contact me directly once you know where you want to go," he said. "Again, we are so sorry about this. We really wanted to hire you."

Whoa. I slumped in my chair. "Is this an exciting opportunity or a sad one?" I thought. My mind had been focused on staying in North Carolina and working for Wachovia. I thought and thought about other places to go, and New York City kept arising in my mind. If I wanted to get experience with the best, New York was the choice; but how was I going to survive in New York? I did know a few people there, but the thought of living there on my own was so frightening. After a few weeks of thinking, I decided to give New York City a try. Wachovia set me up with interviews at Irving Trust, Manufacturer's Hanover, Chase Manhattan and Citibank; and I stayed with a friend for a week, while interviewing with the banks.

During that week, my host friend Janie took me to a restaurant bar in her eastside neighborhood. It was a popular Southern 'hangout' called the Raveled Sleeve. As Janie put her hand on the front door, it appeared to open on its own. "Hi ya'll!" said a handsome young man standing at the door. "Come on in. It's real crowded tonight." He wore an open-collared, starched, white oxford shirt. His sleeves were meticulously rolled back on each forearm, just before the elbow; and he held a bottle of Michelob beer in his left hand. "I'm just standin' here near the door to meet all the ladies," he added. We smiled. Then Janie rushed into the bar to see some of her friends. I quickly followed her because I wasn't going to get lost in New York City!

The Raveled Sleeve felt so Southern. The bar room was packed; there were barely inches between bodies; and the loud hum of voices with Southern accents was so familiar. Actually, it was almost claustrophobic, but yet, it felt safe. I could have been in one of the popular bars in Winston-Salem. The room was dark with dark wood oak paneling. A long table was attached to one wall; chairs were lined up along the table for more intimate conversations; and the bar was on the other side of the room.

Janie introduced me to her friends, and someone gave me a beer. It was too noisy and crowded to really get to know her friends, so I smiled and just observed how it would be to live in New York City. The people looked so fresh; they were excitedly talking and laughing. "I can handle this," I thought.

Between her work and my interviews, we found time to walk everywhere. We walked to the grocery store. We walked to the pharmacy. We walked to the cleaners. We walked up and down Fifth Avenue. We explored Blooming-dales, and then Saks. We spent the weekend days at Central Park. I loved New York. "Let's give it a try," I thought. "But instead of bank marketing, I might as well do packaged-goods marketing." I had met some people with jobs in brand marketing that convinced me to pursue packaged-goods product marketing, where you really get the basic marketing training.

I returned to Winston-Salem to think through strategy for a marketing job hunt in New York City. I looked up the names of the companies there and wrote letters to them. Then I decided to return to the city for two weeks of knocking on doors to get interviews. I met a head hunter who liked me, and she helped me get a job.

In 1978, my first job was as an Assistant Product Manager at American Home Foods, a division of American Home Products. The salary was a pitiful $16,000; I had been making $25,000 in North Carolina before business school, which was a very good salary in the mid-1970s for a 25-year-old woman. Daddy knew how much I wanted the job, so he offered to help me with finances. My new boss James was a Group Product Manager in his early fifties. He wore wire-rimmed glasses and had dark hair that receded from his forehead.

I was assigned Jiffy Pop® Popcorn; G. Washington's® Seasoning and Broth; and Dennison's® Chili, which was the top selling chili on the West coast. James coached me on how to "crunch the numbers" to understand the business and he also taught me how to steer my way through company politics to get approvals for the marketing programs. Management liked me. Within a year, I was promoted to Product Manager, with added responsibility to run the Gulden's® Mustard business, in addition to the others.

$\mathcal{I}$ lived in a junior one-bedroom apartment in midtown Manhattan that was only 17 blocks from my marketing job, which was almost a mile. It was so close that I could walk to work. Every day, I dressed up in my best suit; put on my heels; and trekked to work. At the time, walking in Manhattan was like maneuvering an obstacle course, because I had to constantly look at the sidewalk to avoid stepping in the dog poop. This was before the "pooper scooper laws," where owners were fined if they did not clean up their dogs' mess. When there was not dog poop, I had to carefully avoid getting my heels caught in any sidewalk cracks.

Finally at work, I closed my office door and slumped into my chair. I kicked off my shoes. My feet throbbed. It was a pulsating pain, thumping right along with my heartbeat. Then I pulled out a box of band aids from my desk drawer and covered new blisters.

"This cannot go on!" I thought. So I had the ingenious idea of wearing tennis shoes to work, instead of painful heels. "But people may think I'm really tacky!" I thought. So, I had another ingenious idea of carrying my expensive heels in my hand every day, instead of a bag, so that everyone would know that I did not look like that at work. This was before the NYC transit strike of the early 1980s that forced many people to walk to work, thus popularizing commuting in sneakers. I was a woman before my time!

My boss James thought I looked silly, so he tried to embarrass me. In the early evenings, once I was laced up in my socks and sneakers to walk home, James dropped by my office and requested me to deliver a report to the chairman's office on the 31st floor. Like a trooper, I held my breath and dropped off the report, and thankfully, I never ran into the chairman.

My stepmother had always told me that people judge you by the shoes you wear. They must be beautiful and they must be in perfect condition, she said. Not only do I have wide feet, but I also have bunions on both large toes. This has made it terribly painful to wear any shoes at all. As a teenager, my step mom usually purchased new shoes for me right before family trips. I remember hobbling behind everyone because my feet were in so much pain. The blisters were raw; some were bleeding; and sometimes, the pulsating pain brought tears to my eyes. Most women love shoes, but I am not one of them.

MEETING MR. RIGHT?

A year later, I dropped by the Raveled Sleeve for a drink after work. It was later than rush hour and the bar was quiet. I ordered a chardonnay from the bar. "Hello, I'm Ronald Divine," said a voice.

I looked up: a handsome older gentleman stood beside me at the bar. He was impeccably dressed, wearing a navy suit with tiny red pin stripes. A cream silk handkerchief was neatly folded in his jacket breast pocket; and a dark maroon cashmere scarf was hanging around his neck. "May I buy you a drink?" he asked.

We moved to a wall table on the other side of the room to chat. He had silver blonde hair that was neatly parted on the side. His blue eyes penetrated into mine as he asked questions. He wore wire rimmed glasses. He was an entrepreneur: he bought and sold businesses through leveraging. He lived on Long Island but had a New York apartment, just two blocks away from mine in midtown. He was divorced. He asked if he could call me sometime, and I said, "Yes."

"This is an attractive man," I thought. He was in my mind all the way home. For the next few days, I found myself nervously looking at the telephone, hoping it would ring. It did.

That Saturday night, Ron picked me up in the lobby of my building. Our first date was in a neighborhood French restaurant called La Mangeoire Brasserie; we sat in a private corner. "What would your family say about you going out with an older man?" he asked.

"They would be fine with it," I answered. "My father is 14 years older than my stepmother. So I don't think it would bother him at all. What would your family think?"

He sat back and laughed. "My parents are no longer here."
"What about your children? Do you have children?" I asked.

"I have two girls, ages 15 and 9," he answered. "They live

full-time with their mother but spend every other weekend with me." Ron explained to me that his youngest daughter Jenny was very upset about his divorce, and so he made it a practice not to introduce his children to a lady friend, unless the relationship was becoming serious.

It turned out that Ron was exactly 15 years older than I, and he had been divorced for a year. He went to Princeton, and then Harvard to get his MBA. We talked about our favorite trips and hobbies; he loved to play tennis and ski, and I loved to play tennis. He was so charming.

We went out every week for over a year. We both loved the adventure of New York and scouting out unique restaurants; and we also loved going to some of his favorites, such as Le Cirque, Le Perigord, and The Four Seasons. He introduced me to the opera and the ballet; we played tennis, and he let me win a few games.

It was getting serious. "I would like you to meet Jenny," he said. "She is coming to my house this weekend, and I will be bringing her into the city. Are you free?" Jenny was his ten-year-old daughter. I was excited and nervous at the same time. What if she doesn't like me?

I worried all week. What should I say? How should I act? What should I wear? I couldn't believe I was acting like this over meeting a ten-year-old girl. The plan was that we would meet for cheese and crackers at his apartment and then take Jenny to a fun restaurant.

I got to his apartment first and let myself in. I pulled out the hors d'oeuvres and placed them on a platter; and then I started looking through New York Magazine, awaiting their arrival.

The door opened. "No smoking!" yelled a little girl's voice. I looked up. There she was with one hand on her hip and the other pointing at me. "Daddy, that woman is smoking! You can't smoke in my Daddy's home!" I quickly put out my cigarette.

"Jenny, stop it," he said. Ron stooped on his knees and held onto Jenny's pointing hand. "Miss Wright is our guest. We don't talk to guests like that."

Jenny pulled her hand away; she scrunched up her face and gave me an angry look. "Daddy, I want to call mommy." Then she ran into his apartment guestroom and slammed the door.

We decided to have pizza delivered to the apartment, instead of going out. The pizza arrived; but Jenny would not come out of her room, and so Ron and I ate alone. I left early.

The encounter with this ten-year-old child brought up old feelings in me. I wanted my real parents together too when I was ten, but it was not possible because Mother had died. I felt so inadequate; I had lost confidence because of an angry child.

Ron had difficulty discussing any kind of feelings, so we

never resolved what went on the night of meeting Jenny: he was torn between the love of his children and me. We slowly drifted apart and decided to take a break from dating for a while. I was devastated.

Ron and I got back together, and then we broke up a few times over the next few years. Finally, he chose a television actress to marry instead of me. Even though I was very sad about losing him, I knew somehow it was for the best. I was attracted to older, sophisticated men, but I knew I needed to meet someone a little closer to my age. Ron and I remained close friends, and we met frequently for breakfast, when he was in town. We remained good friends until he contracted Parkinson's disease and was no longer able to venture into the city.

I joined a group beach house, as well as a few social clubs, in the Hamptons where I met many fun and attractive men and women. I dated lots of men, but nothing became as serious as it had been with Ron. My main concentration was on my marketing career.

*N*ot long after moving to New York in the summer of 1978, I went alone to a neighborhood restaurant to treat myself to a seafood dinner. While standing in line, I met a nice woman named Sonia, who was also waiting in line with her two children. She was a beautiful, vibrant person who seemed to light up the people that she was around. She had dark hair with a perfect olive complexion and dark brown sparkling eyes. We chatted and kidded a lot in line, and it turned out that she lived around the corner from my apartment. Even though she was married, her husband was not too interested in socializing, and so after that, I often got together with her and her two young sons, Steve and Skipper, to do neighborhood dinners.

I remember helping Sonia teach her youngest son, Skipper, who was around three years old at the time, how to behave in a restaurant. Like most children of that age, he could not sit down. He could not sit still for 30 seconds, and he could not stand still for even 10 seconds, so we had the little energizer bunny running around and around and around our dinner tables. His older brother Steve was so sweet and calm, watching us pull our hair out at one moment and then giggling the next. That was the problem. Skipper knew that he was funny, that is, to us who loved him, but not necessarily to other restaurant goers. For that reason, we always chose restaurants that were not too crowded, so that we would not upset too many people.

Sonia and I had much in common, and it felt as if we had been friends many times before. We shared the same views towards life and we talked for hours about philosophy and religion, which is not necessarily a good thing to do, unless you share common perspectives. She had an unshakable, inherent integrity that was the backbone for all of her decisions and choices. One of the things that I admired the most about her was that she was not judgmental. Coming from a background where every little thought and twist of my body had been scrutinized, it was such a relief to have a close friend who did not see me as a little weird because my perspective was a little different.

Over time, Sonia and I became like sisters, deeper than friends. She remained my token married friend, while I traversed along the New York single path, and none of my new single friends ever met her because singles and married people just did not interconnect. We seemed to live in separate universes with completely different interests, all in the same city-space.

As the years passed, I wondered more about my mother. What would my life have been like, had she lived? What would my life have been like, had we been prepared to lose her and been able to say good-bye? Would I have been more outgoing? Would I have been less afraid of things? Would I have been more confident? Would I have been happier?

I knew so little about Mother because the pain from losing her had been so deep for my father and me that we must have made an unconscious agreement not to talk about her, almost as if she had never existed. I wanted so much to know about her, but I was loath to force Daddy to open up any more emotional wounds, as I knew how excruciatingly hard it was for him to express his feelings. As the years progressed, a few of Daddy's friends spoke briefly with me about her. I learned that she had been a free-spirit and the leader of their group of ten or so couples, which included organizing their Saturday night socials. She and Daddy were such incredible dancers that their friends cleared the ballroom dance floor, just to watch Ginger (Rogers) and Fred (Astaire) Wright do the waltz or jitterbug. She was a dedicated golfer, so much that after she died, a women's golf tournament was created in her honor at the Cape Fear Country Club in Wilmington. Finally, I learned that she was credited for being one of the women leaders that started a Wilmington chapter of the Junior League, which is an international women's charitable organization that promotes volunteerism throughout communities. Therefore, in her brief thirty-four-year life, my mother had been quite accomplished.

I visited Mother's parents, my grandparents, in Greensboro, North Carolina, often. Every time I went to Greensboro to visit them, people knew immediately who I was because not only was I named after her, but I also looked exactly like her. Although I am (5 feet, 8 inches) a few inches taller than she had been, I have a similar figure with long legs; but there is one exception. Many of her men admirers reminded me that she was quite 'well endowed,' while I am not. As a matter of fact, I am flat-chested. I wondered if I really looked that much like her, how it must have affected Daddy: he was always reminded of her by my presence. I also wondered how this may have affected my stepmother; and I wondered how hard it was to be reminded that she was the second wife. I thought about that often, while dating Ron.

I also worried that I might inherit my mother's fate: the closer to 34 years old that I got, the more nervous I got that I too might get sick and die. How much of an illness is hereditary? How much is from proper eating habits? Once I turned 35 years old, I felt an enormous sense of relief.

I got into therapy; I found a Freudian psychiatrist and we met weekly in the early 1980s for over five years. Dr. Gaskin helped me work through my feelings about my mother, father, and stepmother; and we also dealt with my feelings about being a stepchild. I wanted to dig deeply and face my fears and anxieties, in order to grow into the person that I was born to be. However, it seemed that it took so long to get better. I wondered why, even though we talked about things and I learned more about why they happened, the same themes kept arising, but in different life situations. It seemed to me that just talking about it was not enough; the intellectual process of therapy was not enough to work through some issues.

At the same time as the therapy, I started getting massages. At first, they were the feel-good massages, but then I gravitated to deep-tissue work. Interestingly, as the body massage work seemed to help my body become freer, I also found myself psychologically handling situations better. I intuitively believed that we hold our emotions inside our bodies, and these emotions can get locked up in our tissues, causing us to have the same emotional reactions over and over to similar life situations. I believed that our thoughts and feelings were stored in different parts of our bodies, and I came to realize that in order to work through certain emotional issues, it was important to do both intellectual therapy and bodywork.

While "Googling" the subject of bodywork on the Internet, I ran across an example of what I am talking about in a paper entitled "Massage Therapy & Bodywork: Healing Through

Touch" by William Collinge, Ph.D. There was a case study about a woman who had been a free-spirit as a child but was emotionally closed-down as an adult. She was concerned about her feet, as it felt as if her toes were crumbling, although they were physically fine. When the practitioner inquired about the loss of her free-spirited personality, she reminisced about horseback riding and feeling so free; but her parents abruptly sold her beloved horse. She remembered that her horse had bad feet, and then her toes began to ache. She had been holding the grief about losing her horse in her toes.[1]

I did not have a Ph.D. in psychology, but I was always interested in psychology and what makes people tick. I'm sure this quirky side of me is what later guided me to focus my marketing career on new product marketing, because in order to do a good job at mass-marketing something, you needed to be good in mass-psychology in order to understand the consumer.

My father and stepmother were upset when they heard that I was in therapy. "You're wasting money," they said. They saw it as a bad reflection on them, instead of an opportunity to help me become happier, and so they tried to stop me.

"Your father is going to make you stop," said my stepmother.

"No, Mother. No, he's not," I answered.

"It will kill your father if you keep doing it," she retorted.

"Mother, it will not kill Daddy," I answered. I was finally standing up to them, and it felt good!

Finally, they gave in; they realized that I was not doing therapy, or anything else, to hurt them. Working on me was a positive action, and as I worked more on the combination of bodywork and therapy, I became happier and more relaxed.

FINDING MY TRUE MARKETING SKILLS

After spending many years in the packaged-goods brand marketing field, I finally discovered my favorite thing to do: study how consumers think and develop products.

In 1983, I was fortunate enough to be at the right place at the right time to get hired by Popsicle Industries, a small division of the Sara Lee Corporation. They were negotiating a licensing arrangement with Nabisco Brands, where Popsicle would purchase Oreo cookies from Nabisco to create a new cookies and cream ice cream product line. In turn, Nabisco gave Popsicle the exclusive right to use the Oreo® brand trademark and name in all packaging and advertising. I was assigned the responsibility for taking the Oreo® Cookies N' Cream Ice Cream project through test market, and then to introduce it nationally. I did not even have to do research to figure out how big this opportunity could be, since "cookies and cream" was already a popular flavor in many ice cream stores.

My VP Marketing boss was responsible for negotiating the

Oreo® licensing deal with Nabisco, as well as overseeing a product manager who ran the Popsicle® brands. This was in addition to overseeing me on the Oreo® ice cream project.

Our R&D department created three types of product for the new line. First, we had a gallon ice cream product in the four flavors of vanilla, chocolate, coffee, and mint, where large chunks of Oreo cookies were added to these flavors. Secondly, Nabisco created a special three-inch-wide Oreo chocolate cookie wafer, just for our company to create an ice cream sandwich. The ice cream sandwich was 1-inch-thick, with vanilla Oreo cookie ice cream in the middle of two three-inch wafers. Third, we offered a frozen novelty stick of Oreo cookie ice cream dipped in chocolate.

During my first few weeks, we approved the advertising copy, finalized the package design, and presented the test market numbers to our president. By the fourth week, my boss and I were traveling to Dallas to meet with the dairy management that would produce the product, as well as to assist the salespeople in selling the testing program to grocery personnel.

Popsicle owned the brand names for Popsicle®, Fudgsicle® and Creamsicle®, and it sold "flavor units" (formulas to make the Popsicle products) to ice cream manufacturing dairies across the country. These dairies manufactured the Popsicle products and then sold them to grocery stores. In order to succeed, however, the division needed to sell this new Oreo® Cookies N' Cream Ice Cream product line directly to the grocery stores, and so our VP of Sales quickly hired experienced grocery salespeople to do the job.

Our joint Marketing/Sales effort turned this venture into a $140 million dollar new product success, one of the largest new product introductions of the retail grocery industry in the 1980s. It more than doubled the sales and profits of our little division.

Many marketers may think this was easy because of the strong consumer loyalty for Oreo® cookies; however, a successful new product concept is only as good as its execution. If the introduction was not done right, the entire project could have failed. I hardly slept for the entire year. There were so many things that could have gone wrong. If the formulas for manufacturing the product were wrong, or if they arrived late at the dairies, the product would not have been produced and sent to stores on time. If the advertising had started before the products were on the grocery store shelf, consumers would have been upset. They may have decided not to try the product.

Every department in the company needed to communicate and work together. I instituted weekly staff meetings between members of all of the departments: sales, market research, advertising, distribution, research & development, production, and packaging. The weekly staff meetings brought the departments together as a team and helped us identify problems before they happened. My mother would have been proud!

Once we were successful, my boss hired a product manager

to run the Oreo® Ice Cream business on a day-to-day basis. I was given the responsibility for putting together a new products program for the division. I studied the production capabilities of the dairies, conducted an analysis of the ice cream/frozen novelty market, and developed a formula for gauging the criteria for developing new products. Then I put it all together into a comprehensive New Products Charter for the division.

Accordingly, our advertising agency, market research consultant, and I developed new product concepts, and our R&D department created ice cream prototypes for consumers to taste. We conducted over a hundred focus groups to learn about consumers' thoughts, feelings, and usage habits of ice cream and frozen novelty products. We probed their reactions to many concepts and prototypes. We came up with a few big ideas and the successful formula for repositioning a Popsicle line extension. I loved this job!

The marketing staff was then restructured and I was put back onto the Oreo® ice cream business to run. I spent the first month analyzing the business, which included analyzing Nielsen consumer sales, Sami warehouse sales, and Popsicle division sales, as well as the competition. Then I discovered that the Oreo® business was rapidly declining. Not only that, but it was hemorrhaging. The sales movement per grocery store (sales per point/distribution) was steeply declining.

I wrote an extensive report with my findings, which included charts of product volume numbers that demonstrated the dire situation in the marketplace. I also recommended exactly how the company should restructure the ice cream brand, in order to turn the problem around. I knew exactly what to do because we had been listening to so many consumer groups.

Instead of being thankful, a large group in the company was livid. How dare I tell them the brand was in trouble? I was in shock. This was my $140 million baby! I wanted to save it... not harm it.

"Margaret, if you project that sales will decline," said John, our president. "then... they will decline."

"John, I'm not a magician," I answered. "I am reporting what is happening in the marketplace. I am not making it happen."

It hurt to be denigrated by those whom I respected. My choices were to either play the game and later be blamed when it became obvious that the brand was in serious decline... or to speak out and save the business. I had chosen the latter. A few months later I was laid off, along with a few other Popsicle employees. Many years later, I met with the VP Sales who informed me that my recommendations had been followed, and the Oreo® Cookies N' Cream Ice Cream brand rebounded, exactly as I had predicted.

Like the child advocacy position, I did well in marketing, and especially new products, because I was able to put a caring hand into developing something. The brands that I either developed or restaged were like little children that I was able to nurture. I helped them be strong, so they would not have the kinds of problems… the childhood… that I had had.

I was able to build my confidence, one step at a time, through concentrating on two distinctly different careers. The life lesson that I had learned here was to identify something that you enjoy …focus in one direction, whether it is career, kids, community, or relationships.

Maggie with her father on his 70th birthday.

chapter five

FAMILY MUSINGS

I I went through my twenties and thirties without much personal connection with animals, although I loved the many dogs and cats that lived with Daddy and my stepmother in Wilmington.

My favorite family dogs were two miniature French poodles named Beau and Maurice: Beau was buff-colored and Maurice was black. I remember the first time they were shaved to look like French poodles. It was such a shock to see them in their new coiffures that we family humans laughed, which sent Beau straight into my parents' bedroom where he hid under the bed for the rest of the day. He was absolutely mortified and I felt so sorry for him, but he wouldn't come out from under the bed for anything, not even for treats. Beau and Maurice were really sweet dogs and they were always available to help warm up our seats on the sofa while watching television.

Sceeter the cat came to the family through my youngest sister, Ellie. When Ellie was an adolescent, she saw Sceeter hanging out in the Yucca bushes across the street from our beach cottage. "Mom, if I can catch the cat, can I have him?" she asked. My step mom said yes, thinking it would be impossible to catch a feral cat, but that afternoon, Ellie burst into the doors holding a black bundle of fur in her arms. "Hey Mom! Look what I got!" she exclaimed.

When I was a teenager, Daddy brought home a pet pig as a joke on my step mom, and they named her Mabel. Mabel was big and slippery, and I remember one weekend when I was home from school, she got out of her pen and ran away. Every kid and adult-kid in the neighborhood was after that pig. She squealed at the top of her lungs and ran as fast as those little legs would let her. Every time someone was close enough to grab her, she slipped right through their arms, as if she had been greased. It was quite a sight! Finally, we were able to corner her in the woods and throw some burlap over her... and bring her home. Mabel lived with the family for a few months and then she was gone. Daddy told me that she went to pig heaven and became someone's lunch, which of course, made me a little sad.

Although I didn't have personal pets during this period of my life, I still maintained my fascination with magic and talking animals. One of my favorite books was *The Once and Future King*, written by T.H. White. It was a magical story about how Merlin the Magician had brought up and taught King Arthur (Wart, as he was called). In the book, Wart was taught wisdom by being turned magically into different types of animals and experiencing important life lessons. I continued kidding about one day having a talking bird named Merlin, as I had predicted in college. However, I was never serious about following through with it during that period of my life, because I was single and traveled a little for work, and I did not want the added responsibility.

REMEMBERING DADDY

I lost Daddy to Parkinson's disease in 1993, just before his 74th birthday, but memories of him still live on.

My father was a gentleman. He was admired and respected by everyone that met him, and in his quiet and unassuming way, he was always interested in others. I remember a community leader in Wilmington, once said: "Your father listens to what someone is saying. He thinks for a moment. Then he gives a response. He really gives the impression that he is truly listening, instead of drumming up an answer in his head while someone else is talking."

Daddy loved Wilmington. Our Wright family had settled there over 200 years ago, and he felt a sense of responsibility to give back to the community. As a result, Daddy and my stepmother were among the pioneers who ignited the historic preservation movement of downtown Wilmington.

Wilmington[1] was incorporated in 1739, although it had been settled much earlier. It quickly became North Carolina's largest and busiest port city because of its location on the Cape Fear River, just miles from the Atlantic Ocean. As recently as 100 years ago, the city's river bank was lined with wharves and ship chandler warehouses for storing and trading tar, pitch, turpentine, tools, cotton, rice, peanuts, lumber, and so on.

Daddy's dream was to reconstruct a part of that riverfront. In the late 1970s, he and my step mom opened Chandler's Wharf. Originally, it was a five-acre complex on the riverfront containing a restaurant called The Pilot House, a gift shop called The Brass Lantern, and a renovated ship chandler warehouse that was transformed into a maritime museum. This old riverfront reconstruction project was pivotal in revitalizing downtown Wilmington.

Since the 70s, it has evolved into a charming retail/dining center on the Cape Fear River. The museum was tranformed into a popular seafood restaurant called Elijah's. Now, the Chandler's Wharf complex contains many unique stores and three popular restaurants: The Pilot House, Elijah's, and The George. Its landscaping oozes 1870's cachet with cobblestone streets, wooden walkways, and the original rails of the waterfront railway.

My parents started their incredible avocation in historic preservation by purchasing one old, run-down house at a time. I remember taking Sunday afternoon car rides with them while they scoured for old houses to restore. I was a teenager interested in 'teenage things.' Restoring old houses did not particularly interest me at the time, but I did enjoy the afternoon rides because I could sit in the backseat and drift into my private world, forgetting my feelings of sadness for a short time. I could be quiet and non-social. The days were hot and sticky, and it was hard to catch your breath in the thick, hanging air. The slow, methodical movement of the car put me in a sleepy trance.

"Elizabeth," Daddy said. "Look at this one." He pointed to an old, dilapidated-looking house. He stopped the car, and they slipped out to walk around the old house. My trance was broken, but I was usually too tired to follow them. I could only watch as they pointed at structures and talked from a distance. They peeked in the windows to see the level of disrepair. Then they returned to the car to jot down the information from the For Sale sign, so that they could call the next day to negotiate a purchase of the house. Daddy restarted the car to continue their search.

Although Daddy was a quiet, reserved gentleman, there were times when he broke the mold and was quite funny privately around the family. We called this his "Daddy Tom, Tom" side. One of my most fond memories of Daddy Tom, Tom was when he and my stepmother took my younger sisters and me on a research trip to some New England historic preservation sites to gather ideas for creating Chandler's Wharf.

The summer after my first year of business school, we embarked on our 10-day driving trip. We started out in Greenwich, Connecticut, and drove through some of the New England states. We visited many historic places, including Mystic Seaport, Sturbridge, Deerfield, Plymouth Rock, and Strawberry Banke, and we also spent a few days in

Boston and Chatham, Massachusetts. We observed every-thing, right down to the color and design of matches in restaurants and hotels. Then we had family discussions at dinner about what we did and did not like, and Daddy meticulously took notes.

My sisters, Elizabeth and Eleanor, were 11 and 13 years younger than I, respectively. At the time of this trip, Lizzie was sixteen years old and Ellie was fourteen. Elizabeth had a lot of style and was acutely aware of fashion. Actually, after she graduated from college years later, she had a career in fashion as a buyer at both Bloomingdale's and Gucci, before getting married.

On the Boston part of this trip, we stayed at the Ritz Carlton, and the girls' hotel room adjoined Mother and Daddy's suite. Daddy knew how concerned Lizzie was about being 'prim and proper,' and so he decided to pull a joke on her by dressing up in a very tacky fashion for breakfast. He put on a bright yellow Lacoste knit shirt; he sloppily wrapped a tie around his neck; and finally, he finished off his attire by putting on a seersucker jacket. Then he walked into the girls' room to tell them it was time to go to breakfast. Of course, we all knew he was kidding, but the look was quite tackily funny.

Our last stop before returning to North Carolina was at Strawberry Banke in Portsmouth, New Hampshire. We stayed at the Historic Wentworth by the Sea Grand Hotel, which was near Strawberry Banke. The hotel sits on the top of a hill, overlooking the Atlantic Ocean and Little Harbor on the island of Newcastle, New Hampshire.

Our visit was in the late 1970s, a few years before the hotel was closed down because of disrepair; but its majestic aura reminded us that through the chipped-paint walls and run-down structure, this hotel was at the zenith of glamour in its heyday of the early 1900s. It was the place to be seen by political figures, writers, actors, and actresses. It was later restored and reopened by the Marriott in 2003.[2]

The five of us had been traveling in a small rental station wagon. It was jam-packed with color-coded luggage that Daddy had purchased for each of us before the trip. We were hot and sweaty. We were also so tired that anything unusual made us laugh. While on our way to the hotel, we had a flat tire. We stopped and Daddy changed the tire. The problem was that its replacement was bright lavender-pink, and it was hysterical to see the reaction from other motorists as we drove by them with the pink tire.

As we drove up to the hotel front entrance, there was an ensemble of elderly ladies seated in rocking chairs on the wooden front porch. They were fastidiously dressed in their best organza silk dresses and wearing their pearls and straw hats with flowers. These dowager ladies seemed to enjoy 'sizing up' the new guests. As each car drove up with new hotel guests, they stopped talking and watched as the guests were welcomed and their baggage was collected. Once the guests entered the lobby, the elderly ladies whispered amongst themselves.

Finally, it was our turn, and we knew we were about to be acutely judged. We slowly climbed out of the station wagon.

The bellboy brought up a cart. "Welcome to the Wentworth," he said. He opened the trunk of the station wagon and pulled out our dress bags to hang on the cart: a bright blue one; a red one; a black one; a navy one; and a dark green one. Then he pulled out each of our duffle bags to place on the cart: a red one; an orange one; a bright blue one; a purple one; a navy one; a brown one; a bright pink one; a dark green one; a tan one and a bright lavender one.

"You get the prize for the most colorful luggage," he chuckled. He looked down at the ground for a moment and noticed the pink tire on the car. His eyes widened and his mouth fell wide-open, in disbelief. I burst into hysterical laughter, which then ignited my sisters. All three of us were bent over holding our stomachs and screaming with laughter. Then my step mom and Daddy caught our contagious outbursts, laughing at us laughing. None of us could stop.

While walking up the lobby entrance steps, I looked over at the elderly ladies. They were whispering and leaning forward to watch us walk past them. Daddy stood in line at the front desk to register the family. "Excuse me," said a voice, as one of the dowager ladies tapped my step mom on her shoulder. "You have a lovely family," she said. After all of this commotion, we were still approved!!! My sisters and I did our best to hold back the rest of the laughter until we got to our rooms.

That night, the Wright Family Five wandered into the hotel bar for an after dinner drink and to watch the dancing. Daddy did not like Mother to smoke, but she did anyway. That night, he grabbed one of her extinguished butts from the ashtray. With the black tar butt, he drew a black mustache above his upper lip, which made him look like Inspector Clouseau. Daddy looked over at my step mom and flirted with her by wiggling his tar-butt mustache lips. My sisters and I rolled in our chairs with hysterical laughter.

Big Band music started to play. "May I have this dance?" requested a lady who was standing beside Daddy. We had never seen her before. Daddy was a really good dancer, and so he said, "Yes." As they danced the jitterbug, he twirled her all over the dance floor, all the while scrunching up his lips to play with his new mustache. She was obviously a good dancer too, because not only did she follow every lead, but she then jumped onto his waist and wrapped her legs around him. They kept jitterbugging all over that dance floor.

The next day, Daddy was back to his characteristically quiet, gentlemanly self. But this trip went forever in my mind as one of my best "Daddy Tom, Tom" stories.

*D*addy had an entrepreneurial spirit. He inherited a family fertilizer business to run; but he had majored in chemistry at the University of North Carolina, so he sold parts of the fertilizer concern and created a small, successful industrial chemical business. He enjoyed creating things, and the chemical business posed as a more creatively challenging opportunity.

His hobbies, or avocations, such as the historic preservation interests, were just as important to him. Whatever his interest was at the time, he poured himself into it and worked hard at it until he was technically proficient at the task. For example, when he was interested in sailing, he read every book on sailing that he could find. Then he and my step mom enrolled themselves in the Steve Colgate Sailing School to learn about racing Soling sailboats. They participated in ocean racing on their new Soling sailboat, just off of Wrightsville Beach, and they won first place every year for the first few years.

Daddy also pursued maritime art with the same enthusiastic tenacity. Not only did he become a serious collector, but he also was interested in promoting young promising maritime artists.

During my child advocacy career-days, Daddy gave me a present of spending my 26th birthday in a small, apartment condo that he owned in Hilton Head, South Carolina. This was in the mid 1970s, just before Hilton Head was recognized as a thriving resort. Our family spent many Thanksgiving and Easter holidays there, and it was my absolutely favorite place to go because I loved the tropical resort feel of the island.

So a friend Nancy and I embarked on a six-hour car ride to Hilton Head from Raleigh. We spent most of the next day trekking through the beautiful shops at the marina village of Harbour Town, which at that time, was one of the earliest developed areas of Hilton Head. That evening, we took me out to dinner to celebrate my birthday.

"Young ladies," said the waiter. "The gentlemen at the table to your right want to buy you drinks. Will you accept?" Nancy and I looked over to see two attractive men watching the waiter in anticipation. One was tall with thick black hair and wearing a camel suede jacket, and the other man was slightly smaller, with curly brown hair, wearing a dark green corduroy jacket. It was my birthday, so why not?

"Yes," I replied. "What would you like?" asked the waiter. Nancy and I both requested chardonnays. The drinks were brought to the table, and the two gentlemen followed the drinks.

"Hello, ladies," chimed the tall dark-haired one. "Having a lovely evening, are you?" He had a British accent that was a little difficult for my Southern ears to decipher. "Let me introduce myself. I am Malcolm Henderson. May we sit down?" They joined us at our table.

"And I'm John Stobart," said the other gentleman in a British accent. My ears perked. "Did he say Stobart? S-T-O-B-A-R-T?" I thought. "Oh my God, this is Daddy's idol!" I thought. "This is the maritime painter that Daddy talks about all of the time!"

Yes, indeed. It was John Stobart and Malcolm Henderson,

his business manager at that time. They were in town conducting business and had decided to stop in the restaurant for dinner. I told John that it was my birthday and he was my father's absolute favorite maritime artist. John asked us to pull out some paper from our pocketbooks. I found an old envelope, and within 30 seconds, he drew a clipper ship on the back of the envelope with the inscription: "To Margaret with very best wishes. November 10, 1975, John Stobart." The envelope is framed and hanging on my wall with many happy birthday memories.

The next morning I called Wilmington. "Hi Mother. How are you?"

"I'm fine, Margaret. Are you still in Hilton Head?" asked my step mom.

"Yes, Mother" I answered. "Guess who I met?"

"Was everything okay in the apartment?" she asked, totally skipping over my question.

"Yes, mam. Guess who I met," I said again.

"How was the weather down there? Did you have any rain?" she asked.

"Everything is fine, Mother. Guess who I met!" I answered emphatically to get her attention. "Whom did you meet?" she finally asked.

"John Stobart," I said. There was a complete silence on the phone. "Mother, are you there?" There was another silence. "Let me get your father on the phone," she finally said.

When Daddy got on the line, I could detect a note of jealousy in his voice. "Why couldn't it have been me to meet Stobart?" I'm sure he was thinking. We discussed everything that happened and he told me to take very good care of my envelope drawing. It turned out that a few years later Daddy actually did meet John and purchased some of his art.

*T*he last decade of Daddy's life was difficult, as he slowly lost parts of himself to the Parkinson's disease. The most difficult passage to see him go through was the loss of control over his life. For example, he had angry fits about losing his driver's license and freedom to drive, and sometimes, he tried to sneak out of the house, but things got better when my step mom hired a driver to take him wherever he wanted to go. When I came home for weekends or holidays, we packed a little bag that I had given him from Egypt, and the chauffeur took us places. Sometimes, we just went out to lunch or dinner, and sometimes, we visited various civil war battleground parks during the day. I'm sure this was a sense of relief for Mother, since she had to deal with it on a day-to-day basis.

Daddy chose to leave this world on the day after my birthday in 1993. I was extremely sad to see him go on one hand, but happy for him on the other, because he was free again without the hindrance of a body shutting down. I am very religious and spiritual, and I believe that the soul lives on, but for those who are left behind, death still feels so permanent. I know that somewhere up there Daddy Tom, Tom is looking out for us. Thoughts of him make my heart smile.

Growing Up With Thomas

I cannot even begin to imagine how terrifying it must have been for my brother Thomas to deal with the sudden loss of our mother. He was just a four-year-old child with hardly any understanding of death. Many psychologists say that terrorized children tend to compensate by turning to anger, in order to counteract the deep terror. I believe that, although Thomas loved our father very deeply, the terror that he felt about losing Mother may have turned into anger at Daddy. I may have been a little angry too, but I had to somehow rise above the feelings and be strong for both Daddy and Thomas.

Although Thomas and I were only two years apart, I took on a nurturing parental role of sorts, as well as a six-year-old little girl could. Over the years, we became close, but we also had our issues. I remember when we fought over toys as young children and Thomas was really angry at me, our maid Carrie pretended to spank me to appease him. She put her hand on my leg and slapped her hand, pretending that she was spanking me, whether or not it was my fault, in order to make peace.

When we were teenagers, we had a typical brother/sister

confrontational relationship. I remember when I had a mad crush on a young teenage boy; Thomas publicly embarrassed me, as often as possible, in front of the young man. When he ran into 'my crush' on the beach, and if I was in the area, he mercilessly ranted: "Margaret and Donald, sitting in a tree, k-i-s-s-i-n-g!"

On the other hand, when Daddy and our new mother were angry at Thomas for one reason or the other, I was always the first to doggedly defend him. Something inside of me believed there was a traumatized child deep inside of both of us that needed protection.

As my brother and I got older, we socialized together. I saw a lot of him when I came to Wilmington and Wrightsville Beach for either weekends or holidays because he was living in Wilmington and working for Daddy in the family business. He had made the decision to do this after graduating from both undergraduate school as a Phi Beta Kappa and law school at the University of North Carolina at Chapel Hill.

One of our favorite things to do was to meet friends for a drink at a bar called the Upper Deck, which was located in the Lumina Pavilion[3], right on the oceanfront of Wrightsville Beach and just blocks away from our family beach cottage.

The Lumina was a colossal public pavilion that was built on the oceanfront in the early 1900s, and it consisted of three levels of entertainment. First, on the ground floor, visitors had their choice of a bowling alley, a dart-shooting gallery, and a snack shop. A wide wooden staircase then led up to the second floor, which showcased a large dance hall, and the third level consisted of a large balcony overlooking the dance floor where the band was stationed, as well as many interested onlookers. In its heyday, a large movie screen had been erected 50 feet out into the ocean so that dates could take a break from dancing and stand on the deck overlooking the ocean (and under the moonlight) to watch old silent movies... or at least pretend to be watching the movies. A giant 8-foot sign made up of lights that spelled out L-U-M-I-N-A had been erected on top of the pavilion to let the world know, whether from land or sea, that the pavilion was there. Both the sign and movie screen had been torn down before Thomas and I spent time there.

In the 1930s, Wrightsville Beach attracted people from across the entire country to enjoy its pristine white sand beach, and to socialize either by walking along the boardwalk or riding the trolley train from one end of the island to the other. At night, crowds went to the Lumina Pavilion where famous orchestras and jazz musicians, including Jimmy Dorsey and Kay Kaiser, performed almost every night.

Daddy used to tell Thomas and me stories about his experiences at the Lumina as a maturing teenager. Apparently, the dance floor was sort of segregated where the in-crowd, or people who knew each other and socialized together, congregated and danced at one end, and the infrequent visitors were relegated to the other side of the dance hall. The parents of both sides could observe the activities from the large balcony above the dance floor. Daddy told us that when they saw an attractive young lady from the other side of the ballroom, they quietly snuck her over to their side, when their parents were not looking.

Over time, the humongous Lumina Pavilion deteriorated, and since there was not a preservation society to save it, the entire structure was deemed unsafe and it was finally demolished in 1973. All that is left now are memories; Thomas and I can add to that bank of memories, but from a later time in the late 1960s and early 1970s. Although the pavilion was in disrepair, it was safe enough for the Upper Deck bar to enjoy a few years of popularity, as it drew many people to experience the incredible ocean views from its open-air deck. Our memories of the Lumina Pavilion are now meshed along with Daddy's recollections.

I remember late one afternoon, as Thomas and I were leaving the Lumina, we ran into a young man who was holding a little puppy in his arms. With slumped shoulders and while looking down at his feet, the young man quietly padded past us, as if he wanted us to think that he wasn't really there. He seemed shy and afraid of everything, including himself. The puppy was different looking: its tongue hung out while panting and its skin was so wrinkled that you could hardly detect its face. It seemed uncomfortable in the boy's arms. The entire image of the shy boy hugging the wrinkled dog struck a funny bone in both of us, and we burst into laughter, as a shock reaction. A few hours later, we felt bad about our reaction, because neither one of us had meant to hurt that young man's feelings. Actually, we felt so bad about it that we dropped our plans for the evening and walked all over the beach, searching for the young man so that we could apologize. Unfortunately, we never found him, but we tried.

I could so easily identify with how that young man must have been feeling, as I had most certainly been in his shoes. I remember when I was in either the sixth or seventh grade, before being sent away to school in the ninth grade, I took my first group dancing class at the country club. There was a dance where we had to invite a date; and so I shyly built up the courage to call a little boy named Jason to go with me. On the afternoon of the party, Daddy drove me over to his house to pick him up. I walked up to Jason's front door to ring the bell; but his older brother greeted me to tell me that Jason wasn't home. He did not want to go with me to the dance, and so he had run away. Ooh, it hurt! I was crushed and mortified; I spent the rest of that afternoon crying in my bedroom.

Most of us have memories like this, I'm sure. Shortly after the boy/dog incident, while at a party, I ran into a former elementary school classmate named Judy. She told me that when she was an adolescent, her mother had sent her to a psychiatrist because she had been so maligned by many of the kids in elementary school. Judy had a long nose, and her house, which had been a few blocks from school, was different looking because it had a lot of little elf and animal statues in front of it. Actually, it looked like a precious little gingerbread house. As a result, some of the kids constantly called her a witch, right in front of her face, and this ruined her self-confidence, enough to need psychotherapy at such a young age. I didn't denigrate Judy in elementary school, but I didn't stand up for her either; I was too caught up in my own insecurities, holding myself together for fear that I could unravel and tumble apart.

It is a miracle that any of us make it through childhood and adolescence! We all need to give ourselves a hug and congratulate one another for surviving the emotional battles of growing up.

Thomas and I must have inherited a few Daddy Tom, Tom genes, because we had fun pulling off pranks together. My favorite is our fishing story.

First, there are two general ways in which to fish in the ocean. One way, which is called bottom fishing, is to take a boat out into the sea, turn off its motor and float along with the tide while casting out fishing lines. The other system, which is called troll fishing, is done by running the boat at a very low speed through the ocean waters with fishing lines cast out to attract fish. These two systems do different things and attract different types of fish. For example, the bottom fishing allows the fishing line bait to be stationary in the waters, and it generally attracts bottom dwelling species of fish, such as Grouper and Red Snapper. On the other hand, the troll fishing replicates small bait swimming along in the water, which attracts larger fish, including the Spanish mackerel and Bluefish species, which are very popular along the North Carolina coast.

I much preferred troll fishing because bottom fishing in the ocean usually made me very nauseous when the boat constantly rolled back and forth with the ocean swells... over and over and over again. Today, I do not fish at all, since I have become emotionally attached to a few pet fish. Although I eat fish in my diet, it has become extremely hard for me to participate in the catching and killing of them.

Daddy loved to fish, and he took Thomas and me on short jaunts in his sport fisherman cruiser while we were relatively young. The true deep sea fishing trips were saved for his friends, but I do remember welcoming him home and having photographs taken with him and his new sailfish catches.

As Thomas and I grew older, both of us were around all sorts of boats. Thomas had a small motorboat, and I sailed a lot in the sound off of Wrightsville Beach in Blue Blazes, my Sunfish sailboat. We also went deep-sea fishing more often with Daddy, but the one drawback to fishing with Daddy was that if we went out for two hours, then we had to spend another THREE hours cleaning the boat. Over time, Thomas became more proficient at running Daddy's boat; therefore, by the time we had reached young adult status, we were allowed to go out on our own.

Anyway, as a result of living on the coast, one generally has many friends who love to fish, and usually at least one of these friends loves to brag about his or her fishing skills. Thomas' and my friend Sam was one of these "tall fishermen" who loved to lie, and he constantly bragged about his abilities to catch a shark. So we got together with a small group of friends and decided to pull a joke on Sam: to attach a bucket onto his fishing line to make him think he was catching a shark.

The day was sunny and five of us, including Sam, got together very early in the morning to go out into the ocean to fish. We put out three fishing pole lines and two hand lines for troll fishing for mackerel or bluefish. After a few hours of fishing, it was time to pull off our joke. The advantage to putting a bucket on the line was that it would fill up with water and give a strong resistance as the boat slowly moved forward, thus pulling the bucket behind it on a fishing line. Also, if you had a proficient captain, which Thomas was, the boat could be steered so that it appeared that the bucket was moving in different directions, thus replicating a shark that was fighting for its life.

The first challenge was to attach the bucket onto Sam's fishing line without his awareness. That was my job. I had to distract Sam by convincing him to help me understand how the LORAN worked. LO-RA-N stands for "long range navigation radio," and it is a system to help determine positions of other boats in the water through low frequency transmission. We were using a regular radio that day to listen to fishermen talk and did not need to operate it, but it was an excuse to distract him. While Sam and I were discussing the LORAN, Thomas and a friend Joe were attaching the bucket to Sam's line. Once they signaled to me that it was done, I suggested that we return to fish.

Thomas slowly put the boat in forward motion and Sam's fishing pole started arcing. "Sam, you've got something on your line," I yelled. Sam raced to his fishing pole and started to reel it in.

"This is a big one!" he exclaimed, while standing at the boat's stern. Thomas turned the boat a little to the right, and then slightly to the left, and then to the right and left, again and again. Between each set of right/left turns, he briefly slowed the boat's speed into neutral and then forward. This, in combination with the right/left steering, gave enough tension to make the bucket fishing line act like a battling shark. Thomas was brilliant.

"It's a shark! I know it's a shark!" yelled Sam. He was too excited to sit in one of the fishing chairs on the deck. Instead, he stood at the stern with his knees bent and feet firmly planted onto the deck while struggling to reel it in.

Meanwhile, Thomas was at the wheel and Joe, Tim, and I stood behind Sam desperately trying to hold back the laughter. We looked like the three 'see no evil' monkeys except we were all doing the same thing: covering our mouths with both hands cupped to smother down the laughter. "Wow! Sam has a shark on the line," yelled Joe with a slight giggle.

"Go Sam!" we all yelled in unison. We huddled in a corner on the deck away from Sam, still cupping our mouths and still fighting potential hysterical laughter and tears.

Sam could not hear a word because he was so deeply focused

on bringing in that bucket shark. "I can't believe it," he yelled. "I could break a record!"

The commotion went on for about twenty minutes. All of a sudden, the fishing line snapped and the force of it knocked Sam back flat onto his back on the deck of the boat, with his head just missing the cabin steps by ½ inch. He immediately jumped up and rushed back to the stern, completely oblivious to the disaster that had almost befallen upon him. "NO! He got away!" screamed Sam. "Let's go back!"

Meanwhile, we were still huddled in the corner with our mouths covered, but this time, we were frozen for a moment in horror to see how close Sam had been to being seriously hurt. We looked at each other, "I won't tell, if you won't tell." "No problem. I won't tell, if you won't tell." From that moment on, we agreed that this would be our little secret.

For weeks on end, all that Sam could talk about was the "shark that got away." So his shark tale was indeed a 'fish tale,' but he's the only one who does not know that truth. That is, until now, if he decides to read this book.

Logo of Wright Marketing Blueprint, Inc.
I started my own business in late 1987.

chapter six

RECKONING

On the morning of October 19, 1987, I resigned from the corporate world in order to build my own marketing practice. That day the stock market crashed by 508 points: they called it Black Monday. Goodness, I did not realize the corporate world would be that upset about losing me!

I finally had the opportunity to create my own system for analyzing the consumer, something I had been dreaming about for so long. I had a few good investments and Daddy provided yearly dividends to shareholders of the family business, and so although things would be tight, this was the time to take a chance.

I spent that first year of non-corporate life reading psychology books and studying articles and books on consumer behavior, as well as cutting-edge books that discussed new paradigm scientific concepts. Then I analyzed and evaluated these new materials, along with what I already knew from my packaged-goods experience. It was as if I had re-entered business school because I was working all day, every day, and up to 2 or 3 in the morning. As a result, my new system for studying the consumer was finally born.

The next step was to create the sales materials. A retired news reporter friend named Dan helped me create a corporate marketing sales presentation. "No one would believe a 'girl' created this," he said. "You've got to pretend it came from somewhere else." I had studied a lot of Jungian psychology and I believed that I had created a system for analyzing the unconscious of masses of consumers. I was really studying the "collective unconscious," as Carl Jung had coined it. Therefore, the new sales presentation focused on a few Jungian psychology principles, which I claimed to be the basis for my new marketing system, instead of coming from my own head.

As any entrepreneur knows, it takes enormous effort to get a business established. I tried cold calling techniques, promotional mailers, and networking connections. I was successful at getting executives from a few major packaged-goods corporations to meet with me. They were all impressed, but my technique was too cutting-edge, and so they were reluctant to take a chance with something that was not yet proven.

Like a trooper, I remained dedicated to the cause of finding my first corporate client; but cold calling remained a horrible experience, and so I hired someone to do it for me. But again, getting into the door was not the problem, and the cutting-edge issue was not really the problem either. The objection was that companies were very uncomfortable with 'being first,' or the test client, as they saw it. Unfortunately, I did not have the monies to do my own private research, so my only alternative was to keep looking for that special client that would be so impressed with my marketing system that they would take a chance with me.

During this same time, I read a lot of the current event news and popular business publications; and being a brand marketing person, I became very concerned about what the corporate world was doing to its American brands. Everything seemed to be focused on making lots of profit and selling brands at the cheapest price, which I knew would destroy consumer brand loyalty. Companies were pretending to be making a lot of profit by selling off their brands. In other words, instead of making real new products that would add volume to the marketplace, they were really just moving current businesses and brands around between corporations through corporate takeovers and mergers and acquisitions, giving the illusion of making money, but they were not making "new real money." The concept of out-sourcing and moving production to other cheaper countries was becoming popular. It also was just another way of pretending to make money. WalMart's cheap pricing strategy made its sales soar, which I believed was bad for the local businesses, as well as for the competitive American brands that were forced to compete by price. Everything was short term. It seemed to me that businesses in the United States were being milked, right before our eyes.

I tried to speak out about it. In the late 80s, I submitted articles to news organizations, such as the Op-Ed sections of the *New York Times* and *Wall Street Journal,* but the articles were never accepted.

I started wondering WHY. What was causing this entire country of corporations in unison to throw away American businesses? They called it "globalization," in order to compete on the world stage, but I felt there was something deeper going on. Many of my fellow baby boomer cohorts were being promoted to leadership positions in these corporations, and in the 60s, we stood for more than corporate greed.

So I started reading and researching about the 1960s and 1970s, as well as thinking back about these periods. During the college student rebellions of the 60s, we boomers had been intensely angry at our parents. Our parents were just as angry right back at us, and this was on a mass generational level.

The college student rebellion was fought in the dining rooms of middle and upper middle class families, as well as on college campuses. Not only that, boomers who were still in high school fought with their parents too, and the battle continued on television with Jane Fonda and others going to Vietnam.

Calling rebellion against parents became the thing to do on many campuses, and those who did not agree were under pressure and scrutiny by their fellow students, thus causing strife, among all college students. It was an emotionally draining time, no matter what side you were on. I remember the screaming battles that Thomas had with Daddy and my stepmother, and of course, my parents fought back.

Slowly in the 1970s, we boomers started graduating from college and many of us took on white-collar jobs as bankers, stock brokers, investment bankers, attorneys, and staff in the corporate world. These were the very positions that we had disdained. Our parents accepted us into their corporate world, but the deep anger between us (parents versus boomer children) had not been resolved. We just pretended that the "war between generations" had never happened; but in reality, we had LOST OUR SPIRIT. Our parents were so hurt, thinking that we didn't appreciate anything; and we were so despondent, thinking our parents would not listen to anything we had to say.

It is very powerful when there is that much anger between a generation of parents and children on a mass level. In the 1970s, there was NO MASS-SYSTEM for forgiving each other, for making up and resolving our anger at each other. There was more of a feeling between generations of, "I don't care, if you don't care," which turned into a no-longer-giving-much-of-a-damn attitude from both sides. President Carter picked up on it and in his "malaise speech" (July 15, 1979), he called it "a crisis of confidence," and as a result, he got maligned and pegged as an ineffective president. He said, "I want to talk to you right now about a fundamental threat to American democracy... The threat is nearly invisible in ordinary ways. It is a crisis of confidence. It is a crisis that strikes at the very heart and soul and spirit of our national will. We can see this crisis in the growing doubt about the meaning of our own lives and in the loss of a unity of purpose for our Nation... The erosion of our confidence in the future is threatening to destroy the social and the political fabric of America."[1] It is unfortunate that we were not in the right emotional place to listen to him.

In the late 80s, after studying and deeply thinking about this late 60s/70s period, I came up with a theory on what had happened. My theory was that: we boomers and our parents had repressed our anger at each other into our subconscious minds. Repressed anger in the "collective unconscious" of two generations can be extremely powerful. I theorized that it had made both generations collectively focus on greed. In other words, our anger got repressed into the unconscious and transformed consciously into I-don't-give–a-damn-angry-greed. As a result, both generational sides started focusing on making lots and lots of money... M-O-N-E-Y, at the cost of everything else... "angry, screw you, I-don't-care-anymore-payback-greed."

If someone no longer gives a damn, then what do they do? They look out for themselves, and they fill their own pockets with huge salaries, bonuses, and golden parachutes. Sound familiar? Our materialistic focus on making money then mushroomed into the greed of the 1980s and beyond: greed on the part of the bankers, attorneys, investment bankers, stock brokers, and corporate officers, alike.

As a result thirty years later, our America of today is struggling: we no longer produce many products in the

United States; our monetary system is collapsing; our housing market is collapsing; our dollar is weakening; and our government no longer listens to us. We are caught between two ideologies: the liberals who want to "tax and spend" and the neo-conservatives who want to "borrow and spend;" and both of them demand that we continue to "shop and spend," because we have become a "consumption" society. I am a Libertarian at heart and believe in the principles set forth by our founding fathers in the Constitution; and it saddens me to see where our country is going.

In the early 1990s, I wrote an article about my theory of this generational anger problem, entitled "The Deepening Anger Spiral," and I tried for a few years to get it into publications, including the *Atlantic Monthly*, *The New Republic*, *Harvard Business Review*, and the *New York Times Sunday Magazine*, but it was turned down over and over again. I sent copies to President Carter and President Nixon, as well as former Secretary of Labor Robert Reich. Mr. Reich had just published a book, entitled *The Day of Reckoning*, which documented the steep decline of middle class America. He wrote back and wished me luck on getting my thesis published. Unfortunately, however, it appeared that my marketing system and my articles were being blocked, and no one was interested in what I had to say. Finally, I gave up on getting "The Deepening Anger Spiral" published.

Further, it had become crystal clear to me that I needed some investment funds to do my own private research on my marketing system. I was not interested in seeking out investors because I was not willing to share ownership of my ideas; therefore, the only alternative left was to figure a way to fund it by myself. In this same period, Daddy died, which resulted in Thomas taking over the family business. He had been working for Daddy for many years, but he had a different vision on how to run the business. He changed some policies, including discontinuing dividends to the shareholders. This left me in a mess. Not only did I need funds to test my marketing system, but I also needed monies to help me subsist on a day-to-day basis. My personal investments had run out and I was no longer receiving any help from the family business.

I was desperate. What could I do? How would I survive? In 1995, I hired an attorney to help me sell my shares of the family chemical business, but Thomas, who was far more financially well-off than I, fought it off. This caused a clash with the family and I became 'persona non grata,' and my relationship with the family was then broken off. I was alone, desperately trying to figure out how to survive on my own.

I had been out of the corporate world for too long to be able to return, and so I strived to find what little consulting gigs that I could find in order to survive financially. I took on a few short term marketing consulting jobs, but when they ran out, I was forced to seek out $10/hour survival jobs, that had absolutely nothing to do with my career or skills.

By the late 90s, I was down to having only $700 to my name and being on the edge of a nervous breakdown. Creditor telemarketers were calling me at all hours of the day and night. Sometimes five different reps from the same company called on the same day. Some creditors tried to close down my checking account, which put me in a nervous frenzy for fear that the few dollars that I had left would be taken away from me, too.

Finally, I was able to sell my shares of the family restaurant business at Chandler's Wharf; but unfortunately, I was in such dire financial straits that I was forced to accept a deal that was far below the value of the stock. Nevertheless, the monies that I did receive helped me to continue surviving for a few more years.

One Saturday morning in 2002 while carrying a 5-gallon jug of spring water into my kitchen, I slipped on some water that was on the floor. The jug slammed onto the floor, both feet slipped from under me, and my body crashed head-first into the kitchen cupboard at full-weight impact. For a few moments, I had lost consciousness and became nauseated. Three days later, I had 103 fever and bronchitis, which was the result of my nervous system reacting to the severe head trauma.

Following the head trauma, I found myself extremely nauseated with headaches and blurred vision every after-noon, and I had to take long naps to try to recover. My entire body system was in shock and out of whack, but I did not have any health insurance and did not have any money to get medical help. At times when I felt really sick, I checked myself into the emergency room, which I couldn't pay for, either. The debt kept mounting.

I was no longer accepted by my family and was living alone with my precious animal children, whom you will meet in the next chapter. Although I was alone, God had blessed me with the support from my friend Sonia who helped me through this ordeal. Although she had moved to the Phoenix, Arizona area, sometime in the late 1980s, we were constantly in touch. When I was in the emergency room in the middle of the night, she constantly called on the cell to make sure I was alright. We always looked out for each other, no matter how dire the circumstances.

For over a decade, I lived on the edge, wondering how I was going to survive the next month, but somehow, my faith in God and my sister-friend Sonia helped me survive the travail. Slowly, my life and health started coming together, and in 2006, I moved to Phoenix to be there for Sonia, as she fought off cancer.

Like a weed, I just kept coming back. Although by most standards, my life may seem traumatic, I see myself as being blessed, as well as the luckiest human on this planet.

Photo of Tintagel, England. I spent time alone in Merlin's cave.

chapter seven

MEETING MERLIN

*I*magine being in the same cave where Merlin the Magician of Camelot casts his spells. It's dark, except for the single candle that flickers to the vibration of his chants. The walls are alive, with shadows flittering and twinkling, in perfect tune to the flickering candle. The echoes from his chants bounce against the walls, filling the space with deep, melodious sound. You are uplifted, drunken with giddiness, almost floating...

I wanted to be there; I wanted to feel the magic that I had read about in T.H. White's classic, *The Once and Future King*, and Marion Zimmer Bradley's novel, *Mists of Avalon*. Due to my fascination with magic and talking animals, I was totally captivated by stories of the druid Merlin and King Arthur and his Round Table. So I decided to visit areas in Cornwall England, where so much of the Arthurian legend had reputedly taken place.

My first stop was Tintagel, a tiny little fishing village where they say that King Arthur was born. It was the week before

Memorial Day weekend of 1991. My timing was perfect because I had arrived a few weeks before the crowded tourist season was to begin, and so the little village was deserted with hardly a tourist in sight. Accordingly, I had one whole morning to explore Merlin's cave, where he did his magic, and I was going to be there ALL ALONE!

It was a perfect day in late-May of 1991 for an adventure with a chilling, brisk wind and chilly temperature in the low 60s. Merlin's cave was in a little cove, just off of a beach and under the cliffs that held the remains of King Arthur's birthplace, Tintagel Castle. The cliff walls were steep: possibly one hundred feet deep, about the equivalent of ten stories of a New York City apartment building; and the only way to get to Merlin's cave was to climb down a cliff on some rickety steps that led to the beach. Was I up for it? Yes siree Bob, I was! Nothing was going to stop me from exploring Merlin's cave, not even my fear of heights.

I grabbed onto a thin metal handrail with both hands as I slowly climbed down some narrow, metal steps, one at a time. The handrail wobbled and swayed to my weight as I clutched for dear life and the cold wind gusts blew me into the rail. I held my eyes downcast onto the unsteady steps, determined not to look out at the panoramic view of the whitecaps as they danced across the choppy sea. "Oh Lord, bless me through this one," I thought. There must have been 150 shaky steps.[1]

Finally, my left foot set on solid ground. There I was: alone on the desolate beach, surrounded by cliffs that jutted into the heavens. Large slabs of sheer rock were piled on top of each other, hiding the cave entrance. The tide was low, and the rocks were slippery from the algae that had grown on them when the tide was in. I climbed the rocks, maneuvering from one to another, to get to the cave entrance. The cave was dark and approximately 20 feet wide and 50 feet deep. There were small water puddles on the ground from the sea, and so I imagined that the cave must have filled up with water at high tide. I walked around the puddles into the middle of the cave, found a dry rock, and sat upon it.

I sat there quietly, closed my eyes, and opened my ears, listening. I could hear the distant "ssss" sound of the sea and "shhh, shhh" gusty sparks of the wind, as they blended together into a rhythmic orchestration outside of the cave. I felt as if I were sitting deep inside of Mother Nature's womb, safe and warm, protected from the powerful forces of the wind and sea. I could feel the power of the cave, and I imagined what incantations Merlin may have done in the space. I opened my eyes, took a deep breath and bellowed out a chant from my gut, pretending that it blended with the chants that Merlin may have made. Imagine. I was in such a powerful place, one so forceful that it withstood historic time. The emotion welled up in my chest at the thought of how lucky I was to be there, all by myself.

Everywhere I went on the entire Camelot trip, the idea of parrots kept arising. In conversation, new acquaintances would mention their parrots at home... a parrot lived in the lobby of one of the inns where I stayed. Then I remembered: I had predicted that I would get a talking bird in my "adult life."

Following the trip, I spent months thinking about and doing research on parrots. What were they like? Which would be the best species for me? Due to its intelligence and great talking abilities, the African Grey parrot became my obvious choice. The more I read about Greys, the more excited I got. It was as if the little child in me had awakened and taken charge. With a spring in my step and a twinkle in my eye, I became so bubbly and playful that my friends thought I had some secret sweetheart stowed away. But I knew that my life was about to change forever because I was going to have a "talking animal" once again in my life.

I went from bird store to bird store, looking and finally, I entered Marc Marrone's New York Parrots of the World store. He had a table full of baby African Grey chicks, waiting to be picked for their new homes. I played with a few babies, and all of a sudden, one from the middle of the pack let out a loud squawk. I stuck out my hand and she climbed on; that first connection was so powerful that I burst into tears. This was my baby! I just knew it! I had finally found my African Grey companion, or she had found me.

From that day on, I was captivated by this precious little creature. She was three months old, and interestingly, she had been born on THE very day of my magical experience in Merlin's cave in Tintagel, England! This made naming her even more significant. As I had predicted in college, about twenty years before, I named her Merlin Tewillager Wright: Merlin, after the great druid Merlin, the Magician of Camelot; Tewillager, after Mr. Tewillager, the magical rabbit of my childhood; and Wright, after me.

Greys have a reputation for being highly intelligent, sometimes comical in personality, and for being the best talkers of the parrot world. They are about the size of a Mourning dove, and they have gray feathers with red tails. There are two types (or sub-species) of Greys: Congo African Greys and Timneh Greys, and both of them originated from equatorial Africa. However, pet Greys (and other pet birds) are domestically raised and sold through breeders and bird stores, as it is illegal to bring wild Greys from Africa into the United States.[2]

I remember that first day when I brought her home from the store. I sat on my sofa and opened up the carrier box that I used to transport her, and I put the back of my hand against her breast, "UP," I said. Slowly, she climbed onto my hand; I leaned back on the sofa in my tiny junior-one-bedroom apartment and we just stared at each other, wondering what to do next.

"Hello, Merlin," I said. "This is your new home and I'm so happy to have you here! I'm going to make you really happy!" She looked at me and then bowed her head for me to rub. I gently massaged her head with my left hand while holding her with my right hand. She slowly tilted and moved her head to expose the areas she wanted rubbed.

A few minutes later, I walked around the apartment with her on my hand to introduce her to her new home. Then I placed her in her new cage, which was in the far corner of the apartment by the window, and let her be alone for a while to get used to the energies of her new surroundings.

That night we lay together on my sofa, exhausted from the tensions and anxieties of that first day. I felt the warmth of her little one-pound gray fluff-ball body, as she lay flat on my left collarbone, with her legs stretched out and her head tucked up in the crook of my neck and chin, listening to my heartbeat. As I gently massaged her head with my thumb and two index fingers, she became limp. Sometimes she looked up into my eyes and let out baby whimpers and purrs. I felt so close to this precious little ball of feathers; I didn't want the evening to end. I just wanted to love and be with this creature that was so exhausted and vulnerable and beautiful, for the rest of my life.

The next morning, I sat on the floor, watching her learn to get around her cage. She grabbed onto one of the bars of her cage with one foot, and slowly pulled herself up the side of the cage, placing one foot above the other, one at a time, until she reached the top of the cage. She twisted and turned her head and grasped the side of the swing with her beak. Then she pulled her body over onto the swing by holding onto the side with her beak, and then swinging one foot at a time from the cage bars to the horizontal swing perch bar. She tightly held onto the swing perch with both feet, while still holding onto the side of the swing with her beak. Got it!

While the swing swayed back and forth from the motion of her getting onto it, baby Merlin continued to hold tightly onto the swing bar perch with both feet, as well as the side of the swing with her beak. This helped her to keep her balance. Finally, when the swing stopped, Merlin released her beak from the side, and looked around the room. She looked at me and then proudly shook her body and feathers, as if saying, "Look Mom! Look what I did!" All of a sudden, the swing started to move again, jolted by her shaking motion. It startled her, and PLOP! OOPS! She fell to the bottom of the cage.

She returned to the side of the cage to climb up and try it again. This went on and on for the entire morning; but each time, she fell when the swing startled her. She was a trooper and would not give up, and so I placed some soft towels on the bottom of the cage so that she would not hurt herself when she fell.

I was mesmerized by this creature; she was so beautiful and exotic looking! I had always heard that Greys were drab looking, not gorgeous and colorful like other parrots; but when I looked closely at her gray feathers, there were all sorts of color combinations that were exquisite. For example, although her wing feathers were gray, there were different shades of gray, and as I moved my eye along her wing to the tip, I noticed that each row of silver-gray feathers had slightly darker variations than the rows before. When I investigated her individual chest feathers, I noticed that they were scalloped and white-gray in color with thin dark-gray outlines at the tips. But by contrast, the feathers on her head were light-gray with thin white outlines at the tips. When she sat on her perch in the sun, her body gave off a lavender aura that seemed to bind all of the other variations into a powerful coloration schema. Anyone who ever tries to claim that Greys are drab looking doesn't know what they are talking about.

After dinner that second evening she sat on my stomach as I lay on the sofa to watch TV, and she started to grind her beak, which African Greys do when they are feeling happy, secure, and sleepy. Specifically, she rubbed and wiggled her tongue and lower beak against her upper beak, which resulted in a soft, grinding noise. I watched and listened contentedly. It brought up images of my teenage years when I was first learning to sail a Pram sailboat. When the winds were strong and the boat was heeling, the center board and rudder vibrated, making a similar vibration sound to Merlin's beak grinding.

I felt like a new mom, excited and curious about this new arrival, but yet anxious and nervous about what to do. There was not a lot of information about how to care for Greys at that time, but I had read everything that there was, and it still did not prepare me for this experience. Like a new parent, I could not stop talking about her. When I traveled, I had to show people sitting beside me in airplanes and on trains photographs of 'my new baby.' Similar to the euphoria of a new love, I was totally captivated, and I just could not stop thinking about her. I wanted to constantly be with her. She was so vulnerable and needy, with her baby "uh, uh, uh" grunts, purrs, clicks, and clucks. Not only did she grab my heart, but her neediness also triggered my nurturing and mothering tendencies.

I lay awake at night trembling... with my eyes still wide-open at 3 a.m... holding my breath. "Dear God, please don't let me lose her!" There was nothing wrong with baby Merlin and there was no immediate threat for her safety, but I loved her so deeply that it made me fear losing her. This thought ignited memories of losing my mother, my lost animal companions, my lost surrogate mothers, and my lost loves.

Lying on my back in the darkness of my bed, I placed my hands under the covers and gently stroked my tummy. I rubbed both hands in gentle circular motions, my left hand on my stomach solar plexus area and my right hand over my lower GI-tract. I concentrated on the strokes, hoping that this time my emotional motor would not gear up.

But deep sadness and grief overcame my strength to hold them back. As I rubbed my tummy, I could feel my emotions rev up. Similar to cranking up an antique car, my tummy muscles jerked and stopped... jerked and stopped... jerked and stopped, until the emotional pain was flowing through my body. Uncontrollably sobbing, I pulled my knees to my chest, rolled over onto my left side and cupped my face in my hands. "Dear Father in Heaven, please protect my little Merlin baby!" I cried. "Please don't let me lose her, too!"

I suffered from these emotional bouts almost daily for the first few months of having Merlin. While walking down the street or cooking dinner or preparing to go to a party, sometimes I just burst into uncontrollable crying sprees. It was as if a part of me was so used to losing, when I reached into that deep loving place, that it automatically triggered a deep well of sadness inside of me. A part of me feared that I was about to lose again.

I am a crier, and I believe that crying is not only an effective therapy, but it also is a vibration energy that allows the body to move unconsciously held emotions that have been stored in the body. Over time, crying helps the body to let them go. Many may perceive crying as a weakness; but I see the opposite to be true. Emotionally strong people are not afraid to cry and allow themselves to feel, but instead, they use crying to help themselves to work through their feelings and then to let them go, thus learning and growing from the experience.

One morning a month later, when Merlin Tewillager was four months old, she joined me in the shower. Parrots had to be either frequently sprayed or showered, in order to maintain their healthy feathers, and so I let her play on top of the shower curtain rod, as a way of getting her used to being in the shower with me. On this particular morning, Merle was climbing around the top of the shower, as usual; but all of a sudden, she lost her grip and fell off of the rod. Quickly, I turned and caught her.

"Thank you," she said!

"What?" I thought. I stood there for minutes, stunned with hot water droplets beating on my back. "Did I just hear 'thank you'?" I thought. "Was that real? How did she know the term, thank you? Did this really happen?" I wanted to pinch myself to make sure I wasn't dreaming.

Yes sir, "thank you" came right out of that bird's beak, when she was relieved and thankful that I had caught her. It was not a practiced term that I had tried to teach her; it just came right out of her. But how did she know to say it so appropriately?

African Greys generally learn to speak between 12 and 18 months old, but some learn to speak at much earlier ages, and some choose never to speak at all. My Merlin did not speak again until her first actual 'practiced' word at nine months old, which was "WOW!" There were different types of wow. There was the excited "WOW!" when she was upbeat; then at times when she was a little timid, she let out softer "wow's," which helped me gauge how she felt about the different experiences.

Then she started learning basic words and phrases, such as "hello;" "bye, bye;" "what ya' doing?" "Merlin Werlager Wright;" "cheese," "want some seeds;" and on and on. She was learning to speak so many phrases at once that she did not practice her tonality, and as a result, her voice sounded more like a computer with a Southern accent, than like mine.

One weekend Merlin and I were invited to go with my friend Eleanor and her dog Rags to her family farm in Pennsylvania, and so we packed ourselves into a rental car and headed off to the farm. Merlin stayed in a little travel cage in my guest room with me, and Rags was placed in a pen outside of the house, which happened to be under our window. Rags was not a happy camper and he made sure that everyone knew it by barking all afternoon. When Merle and I returned to our New York apartment, she started barking, like Rags. I had always wanted to teach her to do animal sounds on cue, so I took advantage of her new dog barking sounds by asking, "What does the doggie say?" every time that I heard her bark. When she barked right after I had asked the question, I got really excited and told her how smart she was. Then she learned to answer on cue.

Once we had the "What does the doggie say?" question and response in sync, I started to teach her other animal sounds, by actually introducing her to every animal that she copied. One weekend we stayed on another farm with some friends in North Carolina where Merlin was placed in a cage on a screened porch, where many of the animals could come up close in the yard to hang out with her. We met a rooster, a pig, and a cat, and worked on these sounds. In the middle of the night, the baby cows got separated from the mommy cows for some reason, and they mooed all night long. Merlin and I returned from that trip with new knowledge on how to imitate four more animals. Then I introduced her to horses and ducks when we hung out together, while she was in a carrier, in Central Park in New York City.

Merle's ability to do animal sounds on cue became quite an asset for her, as it gave her the power to attract both children and adults from far and wide, as we traveled together. That's right; Miss Merlin learned how to control the crowds: when she wanted applause, she gave the right answer; and when she wanted laughter, she gave the wrong answer.

That summer I rented a motel apartment for a week in Montauk, New York; but unfortunately, it rained a lot, and so many children whose families were also staying there started to hang out by the window where Merlin's cage was located. I opened the window and Merlin was safe inside her cage in our motel room, but she could also talk through the screen. She entertained the children all week with the right answer... now, the wrong answer... no, the right answer... now, the wrong answer... all week long. Needless to say, the mommies and the daddies were thankful to have had Merlin there that week!

African Grey parrots observe every detail about their environments, and then they learn from these observations how to manipulate. This was particularly true for Merlin as she learned the implications from making the pig sound. She learned that all she had to do was to speak the word, "pig," and she got laughter. She also learned that by just making the pig sound, she also got laughter; therefore, the pig word and sound became her important weapons to thrust upon the crowds at opportune times when she wanted them to really heat up in laughter. She was quite a comic and manipulator, and it was a lot of fun to watch how she so skillfully worked the room!

Merlin loved water. She loved to: say the word; copy the sound; include it in phrases and listen to it, as well as to drink it. On her second birthday, I took her out to Long

Island, New York, to be near the ocean. First, we spent an hour on the beach at South Hampton, watching and listening to the ocean waves and seagulls. Then I took her to Sag Harbor where we hung out by a pond and watched the ducks. Finally, we drove out to Long Island Sound before returning to New York City. As I prepared her cage for the long ride back to the city, Merle settled back on her perch, and then she looked up at me and said very contentedly, "Saw the waters."

I sat back in the car in shock. "How did she know how to make that phrase?" I thought to myself. "And how did she know to make the word plural?"

In fact, she DID see more than one 'water,' but I had never personally made the association of the places being three different waters; therefore, this association did not come from me. It came from the beak and the mind of a one-pound bird! Secondly, how did she know to add the "s" for plural? I had never taught her about singular and plural words.

When Merlin was afraid of something, she started to say "I quit." Where did that come from? The concept of quitting does relate to fear, but how did she figure that out on her own? My response was to assure her that she was "SAFE!" Now, when she feels secure, she says "I'm safe," but she still says "I quit" when she is nervous.

Sometimes she came up with very strange, Biblical-type phrases, such as "I walk with the Water." I'm sure it had deep meaning, but I don't know what it was.

Merlin spent a lot of time working on sounds and phonetic combinations. I had taught her to listen to words by hearing and imitating the phonetic sounds, and she started doing it on her own. For example, I had taught her as a young bird to name the parts of her face, and "ears" had become her most favorite word. When she started working on the "CH" sound on her own, she added it to words that she already knew and came up with "cheers" (ch—-ears). Then I helped her to expand the "CH" direction by talking about and pointing to other "CH" words, such as "Chair" (CH- air).

Merlin Tewillager is not the most prolific pet African Grey talker, but she is incredibly smart and knows how to use what she does know. She keeps shocking me by coming up with appropriate and meaningful phrases that she had figured out on her own. I am humbled to be her human companion.

*T*wo weeks before purchasing Merlin, I stopped smoking. This was a life-altering event for me: I dropped a physical and psychological habit that had had control over me for slightly more than twenty years. Although I had known it was a dangerous, smelly habit, I could never seem to stop, just for myself and my own health, because I was too hooked and I actually really enjoyed it. I had been smoking about a pack per day and I looked forward to my cigarettes because I enjoyed the physical "rise" that I felt when I inhaled. Additionally, smoking helped me stay rail-thin for so many years. I had the perfect model's size-eight figure, which I had psychologically accounted to smoking. However, it just didn't seem fair to keep smoking when there was going to be a little creature sharing my small 600-square-foot space in New York City. Not only do parrots have small lungs, but they also have more sensitive respiratory systems than humans. A bird's respiratory system is connected to its skeletal system, and its bones are hollow and lightweight for flying; therefore, the moment the bird breathes, the air immediately travels throughout its entire body by way of its skeletal system. Further, due to a bird's small size, high metabolic rate, low body fat, and efficient respiratory system, it is extremely sensitive to toxic fumes and particulates in the air. That is why canaries are used by coal miners in the mines; if the canaries succumb to leaky gases in the mines, the miners know they have a finite amount of time in order to escape, before they succumb to the fumes, too. Accordingly, I decided that I didn't want a sick bird on my hands, and therefore, I would quit smoking.

I had heard how effective acupuncture was at reducing cravings and withdrawal symptoms for people who were highly motivated to stop smoking; therefore, I chose this methodology to help me stop smoking. I had two sessions per week with my naturopath for two weeks where needles were stuck in my ears, wrists, and other strategic parts of the body to help diminish withdrawal symptoms and appetite cravings. On the first day of treatment in August of 1991, I went cold turkey and have not had one single cigarette since that day; however, over the next year, I gained 15 pounds, but was able to lose most of it, a few months later.

We all are taught that you should love yourself enough that you would be willing to do something, like stop smoking, just for your own health. Initially, I felt badly that I could not seem to stop for myself. But then, in the long run, it doesn't matter; but what really matters, is that the 'action' is taken. Sometimes we have to play games with our own psyches, in order to get the desired results. One of my strongest suits was my "nurturing capacity," and if this could be used to help me do some good for myself, and the one whom I'm nurturing, then it is a good thing. This was a very important life lesson for me.

I did not become a grumpy non-smoker, and I did not scream at my smoking friends about quitting, but I did make my apartment a smoke-free zone. As I became more protective of Merlin, I learned about other types of fumes that were also extremely harmful to birds, such as scented candles and non-stick coatings. When non-stick cookware with PTFE (polytetrafluoroethylene) is overly heated, for example, the chemicals break down and emit several types of organic gases and hydrofluoric acid, which attack birds' air sacs, and they will immediately suffocate. As the miners learned about the canaries, humans are also extremely sensitive to the same toxins and particulates in the air, but it just takes them longer to become affected. For that reason, I avoid every kind of product on the market that has any kind of non-stick coating on it, because I care about my health, too.[3]

Bringing Sweetpea Into the Flock

One day while returning with Merlin from a vet appointment, a man stopped me in front of my building lobby, and it happened that he had a young African Grey chick living with him. He had purchased her for his son, who had just left for college, but the man could not continue to keep the bird in his apartment for his son, because the neighbors were threatening to sue him, due to the noise that she was making. I checked the man out and agreed to take care of the bird. I also offered to help him find a new home for her, if he would have her thoroughly vet checked and quarantined to make sure she was completely healthy.

A few weeks later a precious little 10-month-old Congo African Grey named Leah came to live with Merlin, who had just turned three years old, and me. Leah was so shy, afraid, and sad to be rejected by her home. I could feel that she needed lots of love and attention. At night, after putting Merlin to bed, I spent good quality time cuddling with her to assure her that everything was going to be okay. She was so sweet and loving back that I started to consider adopting her myself, and then I changed her name to Sweetpea.

Merlin was not at all happy about having a younger sister around that competed for my attention. One day, about three or four weeks after Sweetpea had arrived, Merlin got so jealous that she pulled one of her red tail feathers out of her tail, right in front of me. I grabbed it from her, and she looked straight at me and pulled out a second feather. "No!" I exclaimed, and took it away from her. She looked over at me once again and pulled out a third tail feather. I backed off and left the apartment to cool down. Some African Greys have a tendency to pluck their feathers for a myriad of reasons: there can be many physical causes, as well as emotional reasons, and if this happens to a pet Grey, the owner should have the bird immediately checked by a vet to rule out any physical causes. Merlin's reason for pulling out her tail feathers was quite direct: she was showing me how deeply jealous she was of my new relationship with Sweetpea.

That afternoon while I was holding and playing with Sweetpea, Merlin blurted out to Pea, "Yick! You're lucky!"

I was stunned. "What?" I thought. "What did she say?"

I had never taught her a phrase like that. It was certainly appropriate to tell a competitive sister that she was "the lucky one" to have the attentions of mommy, but this was from the beak of a bird, and made up from her own thoughts and feelings!

I immediately put Pea back in her cage and then took Merlin to be alone with me in my bedroom. "No, Merlin," I responded. "You're the lucky one. We're partners!" I gently wrapped my arms around her and held her to my chest, and hung my head with my eyes closed, just cuddling with her for a few minutes and psychically sending feelings of deep love to her.

It had become obvious to me that Merlin was not ready to share me with another bird companion, and so I was going to need to find Sweetpea another home. Unfortunately, I had also grown so attached to Pea that I burst into tears at the thought of having to give her up. A friend who lived in the building next door agreed to take Pea to live with her male African Grey, and so I reluctantly agreed.

Dale hired an avian behavior consultant to help introduce Sweetpea and Burrdo and to help them learn to live together in the same cage. Just like Merlin, Burrdo was deeply jealous and he would attack Sweetpea, right in the cage. We learned an important lesson that I now tell bird owners: parrots should never be forced to live together in the same cage, unless it is their idea. Anyway, during this process of trying to get Burrdo and Sweetpea to learn to get along, I went over to Dale's home to visit Sweetpea for an hour or so every single day. I was still so attached to her, and this way, Merlin was not jealous because she was not aware of what I was doing.

Finally after a year, it was obvious that Pea and Burrdo were not going to work it out, so Sweetpea was returned to me. The only difference this time was that Pea was a little older and toughened by her rejection experiences. She came back with the personality of a poorly trained "pitbull with wings." The first night that I had her back, I unthinkingly placed both birds on the same side of the sofa, and all of a sudden, both birds started attacking each other and then rolled off of the sofa onto the floor in a brawl. I stuck my hands in there and stopped it.

Merlin and Sweetpea were kept in their own cages at different ends of the living room, but the moment I let them out to play on top of their cages, Pea slipped off of her cage in a split of a second to run across the living room floor and shinny up Merlin's cage to attack her. I understood Pea's viewpoint: she did not intend to be removed from our home again. I understood Merlin's viewpoint too, but I had to figure out how teach these birds to get along because I adored both of them.

The first thing that I did was to place a material "skirt" barrier around Sweetpea's cage to discourage her from slipping off of the cage to attack Merlin, and it worked! The second thing I did was to enlist a very good friend Jane Hallander, who was a recognized animal communicator and bird behavior consultant, to help me help the birds learn to get along.

Merlin and Sweetpea do finally get along, but they are still competitive with one another. Sweetpea still has a skirt barrier wrapped around her cage to stop her from getting off, so Merlin does feel more secure. In fact, she feels so secure that she has treated the whole situation with intellect and a sense of humor. Instead of calling Pea "Sweetpea," she now calls her "Sweet Pig," and we all know that since Miss Merlin has used the word "pig" to get laughter, she means this as jab at her feathered sister. Again, this satirical nickname came from the mind and the beak of a bird!

B eing with my parrot companions has helped me to better understand and see myself, as well as to work through so many personal issues. As a child and young adult, half of me was usually focused on holding myself together, so I would not fall apart with all of my fears and anxiety outbursts tumbling out. I was like an old-adult child in a strait jacket, afraid of any kind of spontaneity because of the fear of what could come out, and then believing that I would be harshly judged for it.

I started to observe how my birds dealt with their feelings. They changed from emotion to emotion by moving their feathers up and down and shaking out their bodies, as if they were shaking off or shrugging off a thought or feeling. In the quiet of my home and with no one else around, I started to copy them by shaking my body too, as if shaking out my feathers. Then I found myself laughing, and becoming more relaxed and childlike, even happier. Could this be? I found myself changing my name from the formal one of Margaret to Maggie, and now I use both.

I taught Merle and Pea a game called "Shake your Body." When I said "shake your body," both birds shook their entire bodies from head to talon (toe), in the same way that they shook out their feathers and bodies when changing their thoughts and emotions. Then I laughed and praised them. This game really helped them work through their own fears. For example, Merlin loved to show off her animal sounds in front of crowds, so we were invited to a conference of over 200 people. I told the crowd that Merle loved applause and asked them to clap for her to get her excited about showing off her animal sounds. What I did not realize was that she loved applause from small groups of 30 or less, but the sound or vibration from over 200 sets of hands being clapped scared her. She completely froze, right on stage: her feathers went flat; her eyes bulged; her tongue hung out of her beak; and she could not move. I felt SO sorry for her because she reacted the way that I had always feared that I would react in front of a crowd. I took her to the side of the stage and started to play the "shake your body" game with her, which helped to get her energy moving and focus away from her fear. Two minutes later, she performed all of her animal sounds, right in front of 200+ people.

I was so proud of my Merlin Tewillager: imagine how much inner strength it took to transform from frozen fear to performing with confidence, and going through that process, right in front of an audience. A thought of having to go through that myself puts shivers through my spine.

I'm also extremely proud of Sweetpea. Although she is not as vocal as Merlin, she definitely has shown how smart she is, too. Another one of Merle and Pea's favorite games is called "Look at that Bird!" It went like this: The birds yelled "Look at that Bird," and then I ran into their room to see them. With excitement, I exclaimed, "Look at that Bird... Look at that Merlin Bird... Look at that Pea Bird," and then I ran out of the room. This exercise was repeated over and over again. Originally, when I introduced the game, I also added in other things to look at, such as "Look at that door! Look at that wall! Look at that chair," (while pointing at the objects) in order to teach them what the word "look" meant. I had also tried to teach the birds the word "crow" and the "Aw, Aw" crow sound, but they never could seem to say "crow," for some reason. Instead, they said "Cr... Cr... " for crow and then made the "Aw, Aw!" crow sound.

One morning the birds were on their playpen perches in the dining room kitchen area of our house in upstate New York, and a crow flew by. Sweetpea said, "Aw! Aw! Look!" I was flabbergasted. Sweetpea had transferred her knowledge of the game of "Look at that Bird" to relate to a completely different context and situation. She was telling us to look at the crow outside of our home... to observe another activity that was going on separate of us. She proved that she not only understood what "look" meant, but she was perfectly capable of being able to transfer her understanding of the use of a concept to a different situation. I was amazed!

BIRTH OF GREY PLAY ROUND TABLE

When Merlin Tewillager was a young chick, I met a few other African Grey owners who were also learning about their new birds. Merle and I gave dinner parties where my friends brought their birds, and while eating human and bird-friendly food, we shared tips on how to work with our new feathered companions. Merle had two special childhood buddies: Domino (and his Amazon sister Cricket) and Mobey. Domino, who was owned by my close friend Eva, was a handsome young male Grey who happened to be Merlin's brother, but from a different clutch. Mobey, who was owned by another close friend named Marjorie, was also a sweet and precious male Grey. Merlin, Domino, and Mobey, and later Sweetpea, became close friends and played together a lot at each others' homes. This turned out to be a wonderful opportunity for all of us to learn from each other about how to properly raise the birds. As time went on, I met more "pet humans," as we called ourselves, and

Merlin's and my social life further expanded with more human and parrot friends.

Then a bird club was formed in New York City, and a year or two later, the bird club chairman named Judy came up with the idea of grouping club members by parrot companions' species, so that they could meet together and share information on how to better care for their birds. I was asked to head up the play group for the African Grey owners. Ten of us met for dinner, and we got along so well that another dear friend named Dale, who was "owned" by Sweetpea's former cage mate African Grey Burrdo, suggested that we start bringing together the birds to meet each other. Dale hosted the first African Grey play group dinner party in her charming New York apartment.

Our little group of ten eventually grew to approximately 25 people and their Grey parrots, and it became so popular that it transformed into an organized monthly social event. Each member offered their home for a different dinner party, and I remained responsible for running the overall operation. Eventually the group became too large for NYC apartment parties, so I found a private space in the basement of a restaurant, which would not interfere with the public, to have monthly dinner parties with our birds. In addition to the monthly parties, we also gave birthday parties for our birdies.

From there, another friend named Susan, who was owned by Chippy, and I came up with the idea of starting a newsletter to help other African Grey owners share tips and anecdotes about their Grey parrots. We named it the *Grey Play Round Table*: "Grey Play" was a take off on the Grey Play group that had just started; and "Round Table," of course, related to King Arthur and his Round Table of knights in Camelot. We put together our first issue, which had a circulation of 300; but Susan then decided to focus on other things, and so I took it over from there.

As time went on, I met some bird experts who started to write for my little newsletter. Jane Hallander, who was a recognized animal communicator, had just begun her bird behavior consulting career, and she was very successful at helping the parrots because she could communicate directly with them telepathically.

Parrots are different from most other pets because they are not domesticated animals. In fact, domestication means that all of the wild instincts of an animal have been bred out of it, so it will be better acclimated towards living with humans. It takes thousands of generations of breeding to take out most of these natural instincts. Our parrots are two, maybe only three, generations removed from the wild, which means that the domestically bred parrots that are living in our homes are still wild, but yet tamed, animals and their natural wild instincts are still intact. It takes more than instinct, however, to survive in the jungle and animals (including birds) are taught survival skills by their parents and siblings when they are young. Therefore, the domestically bred parrots in our homes would have an extremely difficult time surviving in today's forest if they got lost outside, because they lack the survival skills that they would have been taught by their parents. Instead, in captivity, they are separated from their parents at very young ages and then avian breeders socialize them for living in a human home.

Jane and I believed that if you understood the wild nature of these birds, you could better understand why they act as they do and therefore, you would better understand how to teach them appropriate behavior in the home. Our efforts were focused on helping Grey lovers understand WHY their Greys acted as they did and how to work with them.

Alicia McWatters, who was just beginning her career as an avian nutritionist, was interested in writing for the newsletter, too. Alicia believed that our parrots could reach their full health potential if they were fed foods that most closely replicated what their recent ancestors had eaten in the wild. Although we could not duplicate exactly what their African cousins ate, she promoted an organic, all-natural diet of whole foods that would provide many of the same nutrients, including vegetables, grains, legumes, fruits, nuts, and seeds.

As a result of the incredible dedication by Jane and Alicia, in addition to a few other wonderful writers, we were able to build a cutting edge reputation for the *Grey Play Round Table*® (GPR) African Grey newsletter. But unfortunately, given the financial difficulties and problems that I was facing with my family, I could not properly invest to really build my little publication. However, in 1999, I met a talented graphics designer named Chris who helped me transform it into a small 4-color magazine, and we managed to build its circulation to a few thousand readers with a low investment, although it was still too small in my mind to qualify as a viable business.

In the year 2000, Barron's approached me to write their pet manual on African Greys. On the day that I started to write it, construction also began in the lobby of my New York apartment building, which was immediately under my second floor living room. I was nervous enough about writing the book, but to have jack hammers tearing up the lobby as competition to my concentration made this project a bigger challenge than I had anticipated. To make matters even more interesting, the sound of a jack hammer became Merlin and Sweetpea's favorite new sound…so sweet to the ears! In spite of it all, the book was written and in its first year, it ranked in the top 10% of sales of all of Barron's pet books.

I started out my career helping children in child advocacy, and now I find myself helping thousands of bird animal children and their owners as an African Grey expert. Just like the human children, the birds that I have helped have happier and more successful lives because of my intervention. They continue to be projections of myself helping me. The grief, sadness, and painful feelings from my difficult life have become worth it, because they sensitized me to witness a world that needs so much love. And love is something that I can give back. This has set me on my new path of seeing animals and Nature through my heart.

Merlin and Pea changed my life.

chapter eight

MY HEART'S SONG

I I had always felt a special closeness to animals, but
when my African Greys came into my life, it was
as if I had been turned upside down because they
completely changed the way by which I saw everything. All
of the animals in my life had been smart, in their own way,
but I had never thought about it until I met Merlin
Tewillager and Sweetpea.

When an African Grey starts talking to you… in your face…
in your own English language… and speaks appropriately,
it can wake you up. Again, my Greys are not the most prolific talkers on the planet, as there are many more pet Greys
that constantly have complete conversations with their
humans. Still, their incredible intelligence and cognitive
abilities opened my eyes to a whole new way of seeing
animals and all of Nature. If these birds are this smart,
then how smart is the rest of Nature? If they are this smart
in our homes, how smart are their wild cousins in Africa?
What do they use all of this intelligence for?

After living with Merlin and Sweetpea, I became more interested in learning about and living in nature, so in 1995, I found a charming house to rent in upstate New York. It was a large wooden A-framed house with a cathedral ceiling that sat right in front of a pine forest and on top of a trout stream with loud, bubbling waterfalls. The sounds from that stream and the fresh, alive atmosphere made me feel as if I had returned to the ocean. This was a major change for me because I loved New York City and had vowed that NOTHING would ever make me leave it. Although I was not technically leaving the city, since I still maintained my apartment there, something in my head, my psyche, had dramatically changed.

I remember our first weekend in the country. Sweetpea woke up with the outside birds at 5 a.m., and she proudly responded to their medley of song that surrounded us from the brook and forests, which then set off Merlin, too. Unfortunately, it was a little too early for me, but Pea was so excited to be there in the country, with the fresh air and with so much life outside. Finally, after a few weeks of being tired, I figured a compromise. I found dark green sheets to cover the blinds and the birds' cages at night, which made the bedroom dark, and so the girls remained quiet until 7a.m. every morning.

I started to explore the woods area around my new home. It felt like a primordial forest with tall pines and 3-foot ferns covering the ground, a place where maybe the elves and fairies would live, if they really did exist. I wondered. Did I really see them as a child, or did I just think that I saw them? I slowly climbed over the decaying wood tree branches and tree trunks. Some of them looked really reptilian, almost as if there was a giant alligator watching me. I found a big flat rock and sat upon it, and I stayed there still and frozen, just like I did as a child, waiting for any wildlife that came around.

I heard that familiar "jibber, jabber... jibber, jabber," and then I could hear and see the dead leaves on the ground rustling and moving, as chipmunks ran through them. Just as I had remembered, one chipmunk ran across a decayed moss-laden tree trunk and then stopped and made the "jibber jabber" sound. Another chipmunk about six feet away made the sound back and then ran through the same rustling leaves to follow the first chipper to his pulpit on the decayed tree trunk. They sat upon the trunk "jibber jabbering" back and forth and then both of them sprang off of the decayed tree trunk back into the piles of dead leaves. I wondered what they were talking about. I wished I could speak "jabber-eze" too, so I could learn more about them. Chipmunks have always been so precious to me!

All of a sudden, a sparrow flew onto the same decayed, moss-laden tree trunk, and within seconds, another one flew right beside it. It held out and quivered its wings while making little begging noises, and the first sparrow then regurgitated something into the begging one's beak. Since it was summer, I assumed it must be a baby begging for some food from mommy, but I knew so little. I had been in my sophisticated New York life and had forgotten the things that I had learned as a very young child. This was all so new and exciting to me: like Christopher Columbus, I had discovered a whole new world.

I did not know many people in the country, and so in many ways, it felt so isolated and lonely, when compared to my life in the city, but yet it was so needed because the family confrontation with my brother was just heating up. The quiet helped me to get centered and clear about what was going on. I no longer had a human family, but my animal family was just beginning to grow. I could no longer go back to Wrightsville Beach, but I had a beach of my own, with the babbling brook and stream waterfalls, right in my backyard. Amid the turmoil that was about to surround me, I felt like the luckiest human in the world.

My new home was in Columbia County, New York, in a village called Red Rock, which consisted of a long two-lane highway that was sparsely populated with homes, probably 5 acres apart. There was a small village where the homes were closer to one another, but it had very little commerce, with a real estate office and fire department and a few other buildings. I enjoyed taking long walks down the highway to the historical Red Rock monument and back. Eventually, I found my way around the area and settled into driving 45 minutes a few times per week across the border to Massachusetts where there was a large organic grocery store in Great Barrington.

Massachusetts and New York State were so different. Although both of them were country, the area of New York State was so isolated and rustic with lots of forests, but the

Massachusetts area, albeit woodsy, had a more sophisticated and manicured feel to it. I loved having the combination of the rustic with the manicured environments, which helped me adjust to the stark difference from the city life.

Finally, I had settled into a new life where my flock and I stayed in the country most of the time, with long weekend trips back and forth to the city every other week. Merle and Pea seemed to enjoy the contrast, and we had an organized system where Merlin's travel cage was strapped in the front seat, and Pea's cage was fastened in the middle of the back seat so that she could have a view of the front seat. Their cages were chock full with their MASH diet, which is a medley of vegetables, fruits, and grains, along with water and a few toys, but mostly, we kept each other entertained by singing to the radio at the top of our lungs. The girls really enjoyed their car rides with me because they had me captive.

Although I had met a few people in the area, most of my social life was spent on the telephone at night. Dr. Irene Pepperberg and I had met at a bird conference, and we became very close friends. Irene and I talked on the telephone once, sometimes a few times, per week, and sometimes, we had three-way conversations with avian behavior consultant Jane Hallander, who also was one of my closest friends. Avian nutritionist Alicia McWatters and I also frequently kept in touch. When I went into the city, I got together with my sister Sonia and members from the African Grey play group, so in spite of living in the country, I was able to maintain a busy social life.

My days were filled with observing Nature. Since the pine forest was practically in my backyard, on the other side of the trout stream that was as close as ten feet to the back of my house, I was able to observe so many fascinating animals. I loved watching how cautiously the deer moved through the woods. They gracefully ran through the trees, stopped and then froze in place, without a twitch or blink of an eye, in order to blend into the forest landscape. They stood this way for many minutes, which felt like hours to me.

One day, I unintentionally scared a deer. I had been seated on a rock in the forest and I was so quiet and still that the deer did not notice me until after he had passed by. He must have been coming from up wind because once he was down wind of me, he sniffed in the air, and then he looked up at me and ran away.

I started to leave a little seed on the ground around my drive-way, and quickly, flocks of birds found our home. The crows woke us up every morning with their "Aw, Aw's!," and the blackbirds, which consisted of grackles, Red-wing blackbirds and starlings, provided a symphony for us as they flew through the forest trees and appeared to be playing games as they raced back and forth along the open space over the winding trout stream. This activity provided an echo that reverberated through the trees, and of course, my girls had to join in with their clicks, clucks, and cackles. I let them play on their playpen perches, which were located on the screened porch that was in the back of the house. I was so uplifted, almost in nirvana, by the energy of the country air and the ions from the stream. They combined with the cadence of sounds coming from the combination of the "SSSS" of the babbling brook and waterfalls, the gleeful screeching blackbird echoes, and topped off by my girls' joyous screams.

Tanglewood, where the Boston Symphony makes its summer home, was within a 30 minute drive, and I started to go there to listen to great symphonies and jazz concerts in the outdoors. On our first Fourth of July weekend in the country, my friend Mary, who was the original graphic designer to help me with the Grey newsletter, and her boyfriend Marty brought their Timneh Grey Polomo and his Amazon cage-mate Esmeralda to spend the weekend with the girls and me. We packed up lunches and spent most of that Saturday sitting on the lawn at Tanglewood, listening to the Boston Pops Orchestra practice their marching band concert that was going to be held that evening. We took turns bringing the birds out of their carrier cases so that they could sit on our knees and enjoy the fresh air and manicured green lawn. Merlin loved the music so much that she started dancing up and down and around on my knee, accompanied by her clicks, claps, and the appropriate screeches, when the rhythm called for it. Crowds of other music lovers started laughing and pointing at us silly "bird people" and our feathered children. It was a glorious day!

That summer I remember watching an adolescent robin practice the living skills that his parents had taught him. Like clockwork every single day for about three weeks, he came alone to hang out in a shaded area that was right under my bedroom window. First, he practiced the robin walk to look for worms, but there were no worms, as he was just practicing the steps. I called it the "Can you hear me now" walk where he would walk in one direction and then stop for a moment... and then walk again and stop. After practicing that walk for a few minutes, he plopped onto the ground to relax. A minute later, he started to grovel in the dirt, wiggling his body back and forth, apparently practicing sand bathing. Then he stopped for a moment and spread his wings out along the ground, apparently practicing bird sunbathing, but he was practicing in the shade. Then he jumped up onto his feet and started to practice the "Can you hear me now" walk again. This little bird remained dedicated to his practice sessions for at least 15-20 minutes every day.

And I thought I had fallen in love! This was the cutest little bird chick that I had ever seen. I did not realize until then, that animals like humans, actually practice their living skills. Duh, Maggie! They are not robots that have everything instantly programmed into them through instinct, but they are taught by their parents and possibly other siblings, too. That takes intelligence: thinking and feeling intelligence.

I felt such joy to be able to watch many different groups of bird parents teach their chicks what to eat and not to eat. Obviously, this is an extremely important skill because there are so many plants in Nature that are toxic and harmful to certain animals, and they could die if they ate something poisonous. In our homes, we have to teach our pet parrots to eat certain foods because if they do not recognize something as food, they will not eat it, no matter how hungry they are. This is a part of their wild instinct not to eat something unless taught that it's safe and okay.

My girls and I were so incredibly happy living in this house and on this land. It was as if we had finally come home!

What Are The Animals Thinking?

After a few months of feeding a large flock of doves, I started to notice individual ones that came over every day. One Mourning Dove, whom I named Gwendolyn (Gwen for short), inched her way closer to me each time they came, and I found myself really looking forward to spending a little time with her. When I sat out on my side deck, which overlooked the driveway, Gwen flew over to the banister and watched me. She moved her head forward, blinked her eye, and then slightly twisted her head, as if checking me out. As the days passed, we hung out together, watching each other, even more often.

I wondered what in the world did she think of me. What made her feel close and safe enough to want to spend time with me? I wanted to know everything that she was thinking and feeling. Prior to moving to the country, I had been considering learning about animal telepathic communication because my birds had seemed to be picking up so much on my thoughts in our city apartment.

For example, although my New York apartment was tiny, my birds could not see what I was doing in the kitchen, unless they were there with me, because their view was blocked off by a solid wall. But somehow, they seemed to

ALWAYS know when I was pulling out something sinfully scrumptious from the refrigerator. Every time I went for the cheese, or any other snack that they loved, they would say in unison, "Want some!" However, when I took something out that they did not like, they ignored me. How did they know that I was pulling out cheese this time, but not that time? So I started to record how often I heard the "want some" pleas when I pulled out the cheese, and they were right about 89% of the time. To make matters fair and assure that they were not picking up on the noise from my unwrapping the cheese packaging, I placed already unwrapped cheese on the same platter as a few pieces of bread and celery sticks, so that they would hear the same noise for whichever piece of food that I picked. Still, they were right most of the time.

Another issue was that the moment my eyes were opened in the mornings, Sweetpea began to chatter. She learned NOT to wake me up really early in the morning, but she always waited until the moment that I was awake, and then she let it rip with her morning noises. Her sleeping cage was always covered at night with a sheet, so she did not see me physically open my eyes. As a matter of fact, she reacted before I began to move, so a rustling of the sheets or a move to get off of the bed did not signal her either. My only explanation was that she must have been reading my mind.

I believe that all animals, including humans, are telepathic; but African Greys have a reputation for being very telepathic. That's because in the wilds of Africa, they are a single species flock bird, which means that they associate with only their species, and they tend to rely closely on the flock. When they are in these large flocks, they move and operate as a one-group-mind, similar to geese when they are flying in formation, and it takes a lot of thought communication back and forth to operate this way. By contrast, many of the parrots that come from South America are multi-species flock birds, which means that they hang out in flocks of more than one type of parrot, such as Amazons and Conures, and so on. They tend to depend less often on the overall flock than the Greys do. This behavior may be more familiar to what we see in our backyards with the many different bird species that come together.

British scientist Dr. Rupert Sheldrake is working with Aimee Morgana and her Congo African Grey parrot N'Kisi to explore his telepathic abilities. Kisi, whose vocabulary is reputed to be over 1300 words, has demonstrated his ability to telepathically read Aimee's thoughts. Dr. Sheldrake conducted a double-blind test where Aimee sat in one room and studied certain photographs and at the same time, Kisi was placed in a cage in another room about 55 feet away. As Aimee studied each individual photograph, Kisi made comments from the other room, and out of 123 comments, 32 were direct correlations to the photographs. Dr. Sheldrake stated that chances of that happening randomly were "one in a billion." An example: Aimee looked at a photograph of a man and a woman embracing, and Kisi remarked, "Can I give you a hug?"[1]

At first, thinking about this sort of stuff made me nervous because it was so foreign to how I had been brought up, and

I knew that the concept of it scared off many people. I think that is because some people seem to confuse telepathy with "being psychic," but they are not at all the same thing. Psychic means reading the future or past about someone or something, but telepathy relates to creatures communicating with each other by sharing their thoughts. Humans do it more often than they realize, but they tend to call it intuition.

Further, we humans have become so left-brain intensive and we rely so heavily on our verbal communications that we tend to lose touch with all of the other forms of communication that are still working. So we really are communicating telepathically with one another, but only more sensitive humans tend to pick up on this more low-key communication that is operating, either at the semi-conscious or sub-conscious levels for most people.

I scared myself one day when I heard myself telepathically communicating with a friend over the phone without realizing it. My friend Sarah wanted to come up to the country to spend a weekend at my house, but I was really overwhelmed and tired from some intensive work that I was doing. I didn't want to hurt her feelings, so I very politely talked to her about coming up; however, I heard myself thinking to her over the phone, "PLEASE do not come." There was a silence on the telephone line, and then she finally said, "I've decided not to come this weekend." I was flabbergasted to realize that I was telepathically communicating on a semi-conscious level because I did not consciously put forward that thought. I was even more shaken when I realized that she had unconsciously picked up this telepathic communication. I felt so bad because I did not want to hurt her feelings, but this experience made me even more curious and interested in better understanding telepathic communication.

Accordingly, I requested animal communicator and dog breeder Betty Lewis to write a few articles about animal telepathy in my Grey newsletter and I sponsored her in a workshop to help me and many of my Grey pet human friends learn to communicate with our animals. Ten of us and our feathered Grey companions joined her in a tiny city apartment to learn and practice some basic exercises. Then I took a few more courses with animal communicator Dawn Hayman and the "Mother of Animal Communication" Penelope Smith.

I remember trying out my new-found telepathic skills with a house fly in my country home. It was buzzing around in my bathroom, and I wanted to catch it in a Kleenex so I could let it out of the house, without having to kill it. I sent it an image of being caught in the Kleenex, and then being set free outside. I immediately got an image back in my mind of two little dark eyes looking up at me in great fear. "Did this REALLY come from the fly?" I thought. "Or was this just from my imagination?" So I sent the same image back to it of being set free, and then I sent another image of love to it from my heart to let it know that it would be safe. I quickly put the piece of Kleenex over the fly, and surprisingly, it didn't even try to fly away. It just let me do it. I couldn't believe it! This communication with the fly was really happening. So I opened the front door and let it fly off of the tissue to the great outdoors.

I wondered what the fly must be thinking. Did its reality become altered by this experience with me? Does it now see humans in a different light? Is this what life is really all about? I wondered.

A few months later my friend Marjorie, her boyfriend Jose and her Congo Grey Mobey joined my girls and me for a visit in the country. It was Labor Day weekend and we were going to participate in two exciting events: the Columbia County Fair and the Tanglewood Jazz weekend. That Friday night we sat on the lawn at Tanglewood to hear Latin jazz and mambo great Tito Puente and his band play to the Massachusetts starlit skies. The next day, we put on our blue jeans and went off to the Columbia County Fair, my first county fair in over 30 years, I'm sure.

At the Fair we got lots of cotton candy and waffles, and played many games to try to win hats and stuffed animals. Then we entered a barn that displayed many of the local chickens and roosters. Merlin's favorite sound was the human version of the rooster, which goes like this: "Er, ER, … Er…Er" So, I walked up to a rooster and let out an "Er, Er… Er..Er!" All of a sudden, a voice in my head said, "That's NOT how we do it!"

I stood there stunned, "Did I REALLY hear that?" I thought. I must have looked awfully funny with my eyes as wide as saucers and with a dumb look of "huh" on my face because it made Margery come over to see what was going on. I finally got presence of mind and thought back to the rooster, "Then show me how YOU do it." All of a sudden, that rooster let out a LOUD "ER, Er......ERRRRRRRRR!" Margery was my witness!

Since that summer, I have worked at improving my telepathic skills, and slowly over time, they have become better. I find that I am better at sending thoughts to an animal than receiving. When I receive, I sometimes get nervous and freeze up, and then the appropriate messages do not always get through. I'm hoping that over time, as I get more relaxed in my life in general, the ability to soften and let the thoughts come in will get stronger and more accurate.

Again, telepathy is one of the many natural ways in which all of us living beings communicate, with some being more aware than others about when they do it. It should not be confused with psychic abilities, because they are very different, although psychic people are usually attuned with their telepathic skills. Psychic is one of those words that makes people react, either positively or negatively, and for that reason, I believe that the Media love to use it inappropriately. Nevertheless, there is no reason to be afraid of or to react negatively to the word, telepathy, for it allows us to open up and to communicate with the natural world around us.

My Own Survival Skills!

One of my very good city friends Marianne followed my lead and rented a cottage near me for a month in the summer. It was set off from the landowner's house by a large open field and in a private area beside a small pond, which was perfect for Marianne since her avocation was astrology and she loved to study the stars at night, as well as to swim. We got together often and took off on various adventures that usually involved being near the woods, water, and Nature. We agreed that we needed to improve our outdoor survival skills, of which I had few, if any at all. So after reading a few books by wilderness survival expert Tom Brown, we decided to spend a week in one of his workshops in New Jersey to learn about survival.

The city slickers that we truly were, we had no idea what was about to happen. Both of us had gone to WalMart to purchase all of the equipment that was listed on Tom's 'to bring' list, plus more! I had recently had a skin cancer basal cell removed from my nose (due to the horrid radiation treatments from my teens) and so I was not the most attractive looking person at that time. I was thankful that I did not have to actually look at myself because I had a large band aid stuck on top of my nose, and to make matters worse, we wore absolutely NO make-up all that week! Yikes!

It was August in the late 90s, and the mosquitoes and heat were in plenty supply. We managed, with help, to put up our tent and zip it up, so that the mosquitoes could not get in. We also had a secret weapon that we did not want anyone to know about. I had purchased a small battery-operated fan, and so here we were, these spoiled brats that could not even stay away from the amenities of comfort in a wilderness camp, not even for a day, much less for a week.

The course included many hours of instructional classroom lectures that were supplemented by hands-on outdoor exercises. We learned how to make a fire by rubbing wood together, which included lessons on how to make the wood utensils. We learned how to make shelters in the woods and how to observe Nature. But I avoided the lectures on how to hunt and kill animals for food because I knew it would upset me to view films about it. Of course, I was laughed at, but I just laughed along with everyone else and stated that if I really needed to kill an animal in order to eat, it would just have to lie down and die for me at my feet. That became a running joke.

Much of the time in the course was spent teaching us how to identify specific animal footprints and how to track them. This was Tom's specialty, as he could identify and track anything, including humans. Not only that, he could identify what was going on inside a creature's body, including physical health issues, by reading the balance of the body in the footprints. Sometimes, Tom is used by government agencies to track criminals.

I learned that animals tend to be habitual, like us humans, in the sense that they generally follow their same daily patterns, which includes taking the same paths through the woods, instead of constantly making new ones. As a result, competent trackers can quickly find animals, once they identify a well-traveled path in the woods and appropriately camouflage themselves.

Animals are a whole lot more observant than we are and

they memorize every single detail of their territories. When something is out of place or when there is a quick movement, they know that something is wrong. Predators, like cats, blend into the scenery by being frozen-still-in-place, and then they stalk their prey by slowly moving closer, one centimeter at a time, so that their prey will not notice them until it is too late.

My Grey companions had already taught me how observant wild animals were, as they had memorized every single movement, reaction, grunt, and groan that I made, especially ones that I would rather have believed that I didn't make. Merlin makes the "gassy raspberry" sound at me when she wants to get back at me for something, and actually, it is the only sound that embarrasses me. What made her choose that sound over another one to get back at me? I wonder.

The more I learn about Nature, the more respect I feel for the creatures that live it on a daily basis. Many of my spiritually oriented friends see Nature as harmonious and calm, but it seems more like the Wild West to me where every day, you do not know who is gunning for you and from where it is coming.

FEELING COMPASSION

As time went by, I spent more time observing Nature and I found myself becoming closer to my Mourning Dove friend Gwen, when she joined me on my deck. Although she was still too timid to be touched, she would come within inches of me to eat something that I put on the deck, but our relationship was not just predicated on treat rewards. Some afternoons, she just perched on the deck banister within a half foot of me while I either read or meditated. Sometimes it seemed as if we had been old friends from another time, and I felt at peace, just to be near her, whether or not I had the telepathic skills at the time to communicate on a deeper basis.

I also got to know more of the other backyard critters. I placed suet cakes on a little terrace, just outside of my kitchen window, and it was such a blast to observe the European starling babies begging their parents to feed them. The parents took off bits of the suet cake and then placed them in each chick's beak, one at a time. These parents looked so bedraggled because there were so many babies, as they appeared to come in groups of different families. They were so comical, and I loved to observe the many different behaviors. You had the aggressive chicks that were constantly fluttering their wings, begging, and following mommy. Then there were some precious ones that were more laid back, and of course, my heart pulled for them too, because I wanted to make sure everyone got fed.

I found myself seeing the birds, deer, squirrels, and chipmunks that hung out in my yard as individuals with such unique personalities. As my perspective of them transformed, I found myself becoming less of an observer, like a scientist or wildlife photographer, and more of a compassionate, nurturing person who loved the critters of Nature.

I realize that professionals, such as scientists and wildlife photographers, must be observers and cannot interfere with the lives of the animals that they study or photograph because they are reading the natural behavior of the specific animals; however, I personally would find it difficult to do their important jobs. I remember watching a recent Nature show where the crew was filming a sea lion baby in the Arctic that was lame and could not go with the family because he would hold them back from their own survival. After a few long cries, his family rushed to him and played with him and kissed for a few minutes, and then they left him all alone while they headed off to hunt. He sat there and cried for a while, and then he dived into the water to swim in the opposite direction, all by himself. I'm sure he was going to die and to become food for another animal. Watching this episode just wrenched my heart and I wanted to reach out and help this little creature.

One day I was driving down the highway in Columbia County and had to quickly stop because there was a beautiful large grackle majestically planted in my lane. As I got closer, I noticed that he was standing beside his dead mate that had been hit by a car. I pulled my car to the side of the road, and as I approached him slowly, he would not move. He stood there steadfastly, true to his mate, and as I got even closer, I noticed his beautiful yellow eyes... so deep... so sad. They looked as if they were pulsating with pain over the loss of his loved one. I could feel his deep sadness. I pulled a paper towel out of my car, picked up his mate's limp body, and placed it on the side of the road, so that he could continue to mourn his loss without being killed, too.

As I pulled away, that grackle was still standing at his mate's side and I could still feel the deep, heavy loss that that bird was experiencing. With tears streaming down my cheeks, I again pulled over to the side of the road, turned off the motor, and cried for this little creature.

All of us experience pain in our lives, although some people have it more than others. I'm not glad that I lost my mother, and all of the other beings, human and animal, in my life, but I can see God's brilliant strategy in making me experience so much of it in my life, because it has opened up all of my feeling centers. It helped me build a reservoir of compassion that I probably would not have had if everything had worked perfectly in my life.

When I am around animals in emotional pain and am trying to help them, I can feel their deep despair. I remember that helpless despair as a young child and thinking that I would never escape my deep tunnel of sadness. It seemed to go on and on and on, because time passes ever so slowly in childhood, stretching the pain beyond what I think adults experience.

My stepmother used to tell me that I wore my "heart on my sleeve," but maybe that is not so bad after all. If we had more love and compassion in the world, maybe we would be able to better understand each other. Instead of looking at our differences, maybe we would be able to see what we all have in common, which is our blatant humanness. We all suffer, and we all have pain, and we all love.

The same goes for the critters of Nature. Just like us, they have pain and sorrow. Just like us, they have families and mates. Just like us, they have buddies and competitors. Just like us, they have intelligence and sentience. That's right. They think and feel, just like us. Just like us, they are individuals.

The only true difference between animals and us is our misperception. They have lives, as we do. There are families. Parents supervise and teach their babies. They have specific buddies in their flocks or herds or groups that they hang out in. They have interrelationships, as we do. They have squabbles and fights, as we do. And they have their intense love and connection, as we do.

When a critter parent is killed by a car, predator, or hunter, the loved ones are left behind. Their friends and families are left behind. Saddest of all, when a parent dies in breeding season, the babies can be left behind, abandoned and left to starve to death in their nests. They are awaiting mommy or daddy to return, and not knowing why they did not return.

.

I prayed to God that, at least once, I would be able to help one of the birds that got hurt on the side of the road, and I got my wish. First of all, I don't stop and pick up every dead bird that I see on the side of the road, but I do say a blessing. When they appear to still be alive, I stop. One day I was returning from the grocery store in Great Barrington and I saw a robin that looked like he was probably dead, but I stopped anyway, for whatever reason. Then I noticed that this little one was still alive, and so I picked him up in a paper towel and placed him in a box in the car. I immediately took him to the vet's office. They checked him over, and it turned out that he had been hurt by the street gravel that had hit him from a large truck passing by. They cleaned him up and returned him to me. WOW! I could let him be free!

I drove him back to the same general spot where I had found him, and then I walked over to a tree near the road to let him free. It was a beautiful, bright, sunny, and cloudless day. I sat down for a moment and talked to him. "Be free little one," I said. "Let this be your lesson and stay away from the highway!" Then I let him free.

The bird took off immediately, and I watched him fly up into the sunlit sky. All of a sudden, he did an about face and returned in my direction. Not only that, he flew down onto a limb of the tree right beside me and perched there for about a half of a minute. He was thanking me for saving his life! When he finally flew away the second time, I burst into tears, as I tried to watch him fly away into the sunshine. "Thank you, God, for letting me save that bird's life!" I thought.

Did our connection change that bird's reality? I know that it changed mine. Did he see humans in a different light? I wondered. Then I smiled and returned home.

To some readers, I may appear a little weird or crazy because my heart opens so much to the animals, but I prefer to call it eccentric. After all, many Southern writers have a reputation for being eccentric, and I don't mind being placed near them. But we all are eccentric in our own ways and we are individuals making up the fabric of the whole. That is what makes us care and have compassion when we see other humans that need our help.

The natural world is the same way, but many of us can tend to keep it at a distance by not seeing the individuality of the critters. Instead, we see them as a group... "It's just a bird. So what if something happens to it? It's just a dog. They are a dime a dozen. Why should I give a damn about that animal...any animal?"

In his book, *Minding Animals*, scientist Mark Bekoff calls it the "us versus them"[2] mentality. As long as we group critters of nature, instead of seeing their individuality, it becomes easier to dismiss them...to give their lives little value.

The next time that you gaze into your backyard from the comfort of your living room, take some time to notice that little chipmunk or that little grosbeak or that little sparrow. View that little creature through your heart. Think about what it goes through on a daily basis to get through its life, just like you. Open your eyes to its individuality.

LOSING OUR HOME

In 1997, once my two-year rental contract was up on my country house, I got the bad news. The owners wanted me to move out so that they could sell it, and unfortunately, I was not in the financial position to buy it. I was emotionally flattened and devastated. My soul lived in that home. It was the place that made me so happy. How was I going to walk away from this house?

How was I going to separate from Gwen? Gwen had become a part of my family of feathered children, and the thought of leaving her behind ripped through my heart. I thought about possibly bringing her with us, but she had her own family and friends who would really miss her. To remove her from what she knew would have been detrimental to her, and I would never do anything that selfish, just to appease my own needs. She was a wild creature, and besides the fact that it is not ethical to mess with wildlife like that, it would have been morally wrong to remove a wild creature from her habitat.

I searched for a new rental for about a month, and finally, I found one in a different part of the county. It was so different. It was in a farming area, situated on top of a little hill, just beside two other homes that shared the space. There were hardly any trees around, except for a forest that was 100 yards behind it. It was a new home and just like my first home, it laid out comfortably with a cathedral ceiling, although it lacked the substance and beauty of my first house.

I missed Gwen, and so I snuck over to the other house once a week to put out some food in a little place nearby in the woods. She seemed to know when I was coming and flew over to see me. She sat in a tree and watched me put out the seed, and then I sat on the ground near her for a while. Every time I thought about the house, I got very depressed and sad. It felt as if a part of me still lived there and we could not let each other go. Finally, after six months, I managed to pull myself away from going over there every week. Instead, I went once a month, and once I stopped seeing Gwen, I was able to finally let it go and focus on the new home.

I became more interested in bird watching, and as a result, I purchased my first field glasses and *Petersen's Bird Guide*. Then I started observing the birds that came to the feeders, which I had strategically placed in different parts of the yard. I remember the gleeful day when I spotted my first tanager, all on my own and by studying the color and markings, just like the pro bird watchers!

I was becoming more and more comfortable in this little house, although a part of me never completely let go of the first one. It is funny how homes, just like people and animals, can affect us. I do not think the girls were as comfortable in this new house because it did not feel as safe as the other one did. There were very few big trees around it and we had expansive views of farmland. Although the area was beautiful, it did not provide a sense of security for prey animals, like my girls, but we did have fun in it!

One afternoon I was watching from my bedroom window a flock of doves eat some seed. I had such an emotional connection with doves, especially after my relationship with Gwen, and I really enjoyed watching them interact with each other. It was later in the afternoon of a lazy, hot late-August day, and the temperature was beginning to cool slightly after the midday heat. Everything seemed so calm and peaceful. One of the doves took off into the sky and landed on the top branch of one of the tall pines that was in the forest behind the house.

A moment later, all I could see were feathers that had exploded into the air, like a huge firework display. Feathers were floating everywhere! Oh my God! A hawk had just attacked the dove in that tree. I had never seen anything like that before. I was horrified! I screamed at the top of my lungs and ran out into the yard to make sure the hawk had left.

As the weeks progressed, more and more doves were attacked. Three hawks had decided to partake of my yard, but of course, they came at different times: a Cooper's hawk, a Red-tailed hawk and a Sharp-shinned hawk. I found myself constantly watching the yard to look out for the hawks, and when I saw them, I chased after them, screaming at the top of my lungs. Over a two-week period 13 of my doves were attacked. I remember returning to my home after errands to find feathers all over the place. My yard had become a war-zone, and I had to figure out how to defend it.

I love all of Nature, and there was never any intent to harm or maim the hawks, but I was determined to make them leave. I got a water pistol to shoot at them and assembled some rocks to throw in order to scare them away, although I knew that I did not have the throwing capacity to actually hit one. Nothing, including a loud fog horn, seemed to dissuade them. I got chicken wire and wrapped it around some of the bushes to protect the smaller birds when they ate some of the seed and suet.

When I returned to the house one afternoon, I found the Sharp-shinned hawk caught in the bushes behind the chicken wire. As I walked closer to the bushes, he panicked and frantically tried to get out of the chicken wire cover. He struggled more and more, and finally he was able to squeeze his way out between the bush and chicken wire fence. Again, I had no intent to harm him, but I did feel a sense of satisfaction that for once, he could feel fear... the kind of fear that predators instill in their prey when they are stalking them.

I knew that as long as I continued to put out seed, the birds would continue to come, and then the mass death of so many from the same flock would be my fault. So I stopped feeding, but the birds came to my yard anyway, just to hang out. The hawks kept coming, too. I remember watching the doves perching outside and then leaving in unison, when they saw the hawks flying from a distance in our direction. They seemed disgusted and tired of being chased all of the time. I could almost hear them saying, "Not that jerk again. Leave us alone!"

Merlin and Pea were also feeling the tension. They had become friends with some of the birds in the yard, and they were forced to witness them being massacred. I constantly reminded them that they were safe.

Like many bird lovers, I had become so enchanted and involved with feeding the birds outside that I had caused the situation. I had set up a McDonald's fast-food restaurant for the hawks, and no matter how much I tried to stop it, the hawks always won. I learned a valuable lesson from that experience. I learned the importance of feeding the backyard birds in smaller quantities so that only the ones that naturally come to the yard are fed. If I put out too much, which draws larger flocks, it will also attract the unwanted predators, which is not fair to the prey birds, as it unnaturally sets them up to be attacked and killed, possibly before their time. The ideal situation would be to landscape the yard so that the birds could forage naturally.

It felt as if I were being attacked from every direction. My savings were about to dry up, and the battle with my brother was in full force. I was desperately working at survival from all fronts. I always made sure that my rent and utilities were paid, and I did this by paying in advance for many months upfront. What was left was used for grocery and gas expenses, for as long as I could stretch it. My perfect credit had been ruined, however, and creditors were calling me at all hours. I was desperately depressed at times, and had it not been for my friends and my dear animal children, I might not have survived.

I had been trying to find consulting jobs, but there was not really any commerce in the area to support me, and so I took on some substitute teaching jobs in the local schools. Substitute teaching became very difficult, however, because I never knew whether or not I was going to be called for a job until 7:30 a.m. that morning. In order to be ready to go at that time, I had to get up every single morning at 5:30, whether or not they called, in order to be dressed, as well as to have the girls all set up in their day cages, which included a long process of washing and preparing fresh vegetables and other goodies for their food bowls. Nevertheless, the occasional substitute teaching jobs helped me to muddle through and stretch the time that I could continue to live in the country.

Besides, good things were also happening in that same time. The reputation of the *Grey Play Round Table* newsletter was growing, and I was becoming better known in the pet bird world. People started calling me to help them with their pet Greys, which was so thrilling because I loved the species so much that I felt as if I were the Godmother for all African Grey parrots. I also worked very closely with my friends, Jane Hallander and Alicia McWatters, not only by including their articles in the newsletter, but they taught me so much about behavior and nutrition.

Our New York City African Grey play group had become so successful that we had broken off from the NYC bird club to become our own entity. It served as a great venue for socializing our birds, as well as us humans, and it provided a forum for us to teach each other how to better care for our pet African Grey birds. Through the GPR newsletter, I then promoted the idea of having other *Grey Play Round Table* social groups in other cities and towns across the country.

I met Nancy, one of my great friends in the country, because she had been a GPR subscriber and wanted to start a GPR social group in Columbia County. Nancy and her husband Alvin had an African Grey named Alexia and a Cockatoo named JJ, as well as many small finches. One of my friends in New York City could no longer care for her Grey,

Twia Kazuku. Nancy and Alvin agreed to take Twia in to live with them, which started her career of rescuing and re-homing pet birds.

Our little Columbia County social group started out as five people, and over five years, it grew into 15 members before it was finally split into two groups, so that we could keep the memberships small. We met monthly at each others' homes with our birds, and then we brought both groups together for special occasions, such as birthday and Christmas holiday parties.

The Grey Round Table social groups usually consisted of we humans hanging out around the kitchen table eating snacks and drinking coffee while bragging about our parrot children, as well as sharing tips and ideas for better handling them. The Greys were placed near us in the same room, but they were together, either on little portable perches or in small portable cages in an area where they could hang out, talk, and preen together.

One of the Greys of a group member had been constantly climbing off of his cage and wandering around the house. Our discussion on one particular day focused on laughing about ways in which our birds had climbed off of their cages and how we stopped them from doing it. Interestingly, that afternoon following the group get-together, every single bird that had been to the play group meeting started to climb off of his own cage at home, all afternoon long. It was so funny! It was as if they had been listening to us at the meeting and were sharing their OWN ideas and tips on how to climb off of their cages. That day made every single human group member a die-hard believer of animal intelligence and telepathy!

My social life expanded with new human and bird friends, and the girls had individual play dates with their parrot buddies. Congo Grey Robbie, one the girls' buddies, occasionally stayed with us while her human Mike traveled.

In 2000, my graphics designer friend Chris helped me to redesign the newsletter into a small 4-color magazine, and another computer programmer friend Carl helped me to create our Grey Play website, which added even more exposure to the magazine.

Then in the fall of 2000, I was invited to give my first major speech on African Greys to the Long Island Parrot Society (LIPS). "Oh no!" I thought. "Here I go again!" I had successfully presented in my child advocacy days, and then in my corporate branding days, but I was still nervous and anxious about getting up there on stage in front of all of those people! "What if I fall apart this time? What if I have a heart attack and die, right on stage? What if I forget my words?" I thought.

I wanted to back out. I wanted to crawl into a hole with my birds and let the world go by. I wanted to run away! Life was carving out a third career for me, and I knew I had to take the responsibility and stand up to the plate, but I was so anxious and nervous about it. "Why me, God?" I thought. "Why are you pushing me out there again?"

Like the soldier that I had become at six years old, I worked through my fears every day. Every time the thought of the speech came up, I sloughed off my fears and reminded myself that the birds needed me. I focused on happy thoughts and practiced my new slide presentation over and over again.

It was emotionally draining to have to work through so much fear every time that I had to be in front of an audience, and I wished for the day when I would actually look forward to speaking in public. So I decided to use this experience to help me continue to build confidence. I started thinking about the birds. I had already witnessed Merlin work through her fears on stage by playing the "Shake your body" game with me, and we successfully got through that incident together, but I was not the main presenter that day. "So what," I told myself. "You got up there on stage with Merlin. That was the first step. Now, look at how that game had helped her. What can you learn from it that applies to you?"

A few days before the presentation, I drove the birds back to the city to stay in our NYC apartment, and then I spent hours every day practicing. The day of the presentation, I drove out to Long Island with a few bottles of spring water that had been doctored with Rescue Remedy to help me remain calm. Minutes before the speech, I went off to the side to stretch and then I pretended to be Merlin playing the "Shake your Body" game. I just shook and shook my body. Thank God that no one saw me, but I looked so funny to myself that it relaxed me and made me laugh. Then I imagined my legs being very long and my feet being dug deeply into the ground, which helped me to feel more grounded. I gave the speech, and then, I drove back to the city that night, relaxed and thankful that it had gone well. I gave my birdie babies a hug and slept well that night.

My birds had taught me how to relax. They had taught me that if I were extremely nervous or upset about something, all I needed to do was to pretend that I was shaking out my feathers, just like a bird. Shake that head: shake, shake, shake! Twist and turn all of those limbs until you realize how absolutely ridiculous you look... and then laugh!

In spite of everything in my life that was trying to drag me down, I kept getting back onto my feet. As I stood up to each obstacle, I got a little wiser and a little stronger.

2001 was going to be an exciting year!

9 / 11

*J*t seemed that 2001 was going to be a very good year for me! My book on African Greys was going to be released by Barron's into all of the pet stores during that spring, and my African Grey website, with its generic name of African Greys, was giving my little magazine lots of exposure. I had also taken the risk in late 2000 to have my small business, Equatorial Group, sponsor and organize the first ever national conference on African Grey parrots that would be held in the fall of 2001.

The Atlanta Grey Play Round Table social group had agreed to help me organize the conference, which would be held in Atlanta over the weekend of September 14, 2001. We had interviewed many hotels in 2000, and finally, we signed a contract with a Hilton Hotel in the area. Many recognized bird experts agreed to present at the three-day conference. We were hoping that at least 300 people would attend, since there were so many dedicated African Grey pet human owners in the country. I was hoping that somehow, all of this activity would finally help me build the African Grey magazine into a business that could support me, as well as help many Greys.

I had made the decision that this would be my last year in the country, if I could not make the magazine and website businesses successful. The owner of my second country home did not renew the lease in 2000 because she wanted to sell the house, but the good news was that I had found a charming log cabin to rent that was in the middle of some woods on an estate. The girls and I moved into the cabin during the late spring of 2000; it was a very grounding place for us to live, especially while working on building the magazine and organizing the conference.

Living in a log cabin had always been one of my wishes because I loved having the bushes and trees surround me. This must have related unconsciously to my childhood when I was so happy, hiding out in the bushes in my grandmother's garden, and playing in the wooded lot that was next door to my childhood home. Before Mother died, I was so secure and happy, and everything about my life had been magical. I dreamed about being back in that emotional place when I was a confident and happy child hugging my rabbit buddies, Mr. and Mrs. Tewillager, a time when I just knew that I was going to turn into someone that was going to help the world and all of its creatures.

It was a large log cabin with a second floor that had two bedrooms and a bathroom, plus an interior balcony that overlooked the living room. The walls were made up of logs; they were not insulated, which meant high heating expenses and the fact that we could not live there during the freezing winter months. That was okay because we had the NYC apartment in which to hunker for the winter season.

The cabin felt so cozy and dark with the pine trees on the outside and the dark log walls on the inside. The living room had a large bay window, which allowed some sunlight to come in; therefore, the cabin had enough brightness to balance out some of the dark interior.

I am a lover of loud, rhythmic music, and so one of the best features of living in the log cabin was that there were open spaces in the walls between rooms, so that I could place stereo speakers throughout the downstairs level of the cabin. I could freely dance and sing at the top of my lungs, while preparing dinner for the girls and me.

Music was more than music to me. It goes back to my teenage years when it opened my heart and emotional center and allowed me to release my sadness, fear, and loneliness into the vibration of the songs. This was similar to what the ocean also did for me as a teenager in the summers with the ions bringing in good positive energy, and the smell and sounds from the rolling ocean waves providing a grounding force.

I seemed to go in waves with music preferences. Sometimes I liked quiet spiritual music, jazz, and opera, and sometimes I loved the more energetic sounds of R&B. My taste had been widening as I became exposed to a lot of African music, which was initiated because I wanted to learn more about

Africa, the home of my feathered children's parrot ancestors. A friend of mine named Mike, who was the proud pet human of African Grey Robbie, had been a radio DJ as a side to his home contractor business, and he had many CD's that contained African music.

Although I had never learned to play any kind of musical instrument before this time, I attempted to learn how to play a Djembe, which is a handmade African drum that is played by the West African peoples in their village drumming ceremonies. Unfortunately though, my drumming career was short-lived because Merlin and Sweetpea were unnerved by the loud sounds and vibration coming from my drumming practice sessions, and so I had to stop. Instead, I continued my fascination through reading about the culture and listening to the music CD's.

A few years earlier, Mike had introduced me to the work of Babatunde (Baba) Olatunji[1], an incredible musician from Nigeria who was primarily responsible for introducing African culture and drumming to the United States. Baba was my first drumming teacher; in the summer of 2000, he held a drumming seminar at the Kripalu Center in western Massachusetts, which was only a 30-minute drive from my home. Mike had let me use one of his drums for the seminar, and so I joined a group of approximately 30 other aspiring drummers, most of whom were far more proficient than I.

I remember when Baba first walked into the room. He wore a flowing white African tunic robe, and his big personality lit up the room. He had an effervescent, spirited voice, and his broad smile took over his entire face, so that I could only see his big white teeth that stood out from his dark African skin. His eyes lit up as he talked about his childhood in a Yoruban village in Nigeria; and his agile body seemed to flow rhythmically as he taught us how drumming music was the vibration of the soul of everything, including Mother Earth. I knew that I was sitting in the room with a powerful spiritual man who was the "earth self" of a highly evolved spirit.

Baba spent the first few hours of the seminar telling us stories and educating us on some of the African tenets; then he taught us some basic drumming strokes. Later in the morning, the class was broken into two general groups with one group learning the steps to a tribal dance, and the other group was taught to drum a tribal song. In the remainder of the seminar, we drummers drummed while the dancers performed their new-learned steps to our harmonic vibrations.

I knew diddley squat about drumming, but that did not matter because no one could hear the individual among the plethora of sound coming from that room. I just sat there, looking like I knew what I was doing while watching everyone else, to make sure that I was doing something right. In a room like that, I sounded professional! Yeah, what an illusion, but it felt good!

At the end of the seminar, I introduced myself to Baba. Since he was from equatorial Africa, I asked him if he was familiar with African Grey parrots. His eyes lit up. "You know the Grey parrot, do you?" he said.

"Yes, I do. I wrote a book on them," I replied

"They hold spiritual secrets." He stopped and smiled.

"I know," I replied and beamed a smile right back at him. "May I have your autograph?"

"I will for the one who knows the Grey parrot," he answered. He wrote: "To Maggie, ONE LOVE! Baba."

Baba believed that the vibration of LOVE held the key to everything. The entire weekend was so invigorating that I felt as if I had floated home on a very high cloud on that Sunday evening.

Baba was one of Mike's idols, and since they shared the same birth date of April 7th, I decided to take Mike in the spring of 2001 to a tribute celebration for Baba that was to be held in Middleton, New York, to celebrate Baba's 74th birthday. The celebration lasted for two days. Drummers, who were either past students or were influenced by Baba's work but not actual students, traveled from across the country to have the honor of performing for a set time in tribute to Baba. Some seemed much better than others, but what did I know?

That Saturday evening, Baba and his group performed. The energy in the auditorium had been lazy and slow, with individual couples and groups listening to their favorite drumming circle friends; but Baba's performance pulled us all together as a group of one, swaying in waves, back and forth, feeling joyous to witness another live performance by Olatunji. The rhythmic beat of their drums exploded into the room; the auditorium walls pulsated, in and out; and the atmosphere was crisp and alive. People were sitting forward in attention and on the edge of their chairs, as if they had been awakened by the splash of icy cold, vibrant water.

At the end of the performance, Mike and I begged our way backstage. I told the guard that Mike shared the same birthday with Baba, and so he finally let us in. We wished Baba a happy birthday and then talked with his band members, who remembered me from a recent drumming seminar at the Omega Institute. I was particularly excited to meet Professor Akiwowo, Baba's cousin, close friend, and organizer, because I wanted to explore the possibility of bringing Baba to Atlanta to perform at my African Grey conference that fall. The professor was excited about the idea and promised that he would call me the following week, after checking out Baba's schedule.

As promised, I got the anticipated call from Professor Akiwowo, and it turned out that Baba's schedule was open for that weekend. Now, how was I going to pay for it? It was far too expensive to bring him by myself, just for a Saturday evening conference banquet. The thrust of my conference was to teach African Grey pet owners about the wild nature of their Greys, so that they would better understand WHY the parrots act as they do in their human homes, making the pet humans better able to work with their birds' behavior. The idea of providing African drumming entertainment, and even more specially, of introducing them to the presence of Babatunde Olatunji, seemed so right to me. But how could I get him there?

Then I remembered that Baba's drumming career had cata-pulted onto the musical scene while he was attending Morehouse College in Atlanta, and ... Atlanta was going to be the base for the conference! So I contacted the college president's office to propose the idea of the college putting on an Olatunji tribute fundraiser for the weekend of my conference, which could be good publicity for them. Baba was suffering with diabetes, and I had a premonition that he might not be able to continue performing much longer.

A tribute at the place where he had started his musical career would have provided a spiritual "coming of full circle" for Baba; therefore, it seemed so right that the college should do it for him, whether or not it was done on that particular September weekend. He had certainly given them lots of public relations exposure; it seemed right that they should do something for him in return. I tried to contact his celebri-ty friends to help me persuade the staff at Morehouse. Here I was, this shy person, picking up the phone and trying to locate people like Santana and Mickey Hart. What was I thinking? Had I lost it? Why would they bother to speak with me? It was difficult getting through websites and agents to reach these celebrities, but actually, to my surprise, the brother of one of them did return my call!

Unfortunately, the college turned the idea down, and so instead, I was forced to find a local drumming circle group to agree to perform for our banquet. I was disappointed that the Morehouse tribute idea did not work out, but I was real-ly proud of myself for making the effort anyway. Little did I realize at the time that my conference was NOT going to happen either, on that weekend of September 14th, 2001.

*J*oy! Joy! My friend Dr. Irene Pepperberg (Dr. P, as I affectionately call her) had returned from Arizona to live in the Boston area, in order to work on a special project with MIT. Boston was only 3 hours away from upstate New York, and so this meant that I was going to be able to see lots of her, instead of just having long, weekly telephone conversations. Besides birding, one of our favorite things to do together when she came to visit was to hike to the top of Bash-Bish Falls in Mt. Washington State Park, Massachusetts, just 35 minutes from my home.

Before leaving for the falls, Irene and I prepared our lunch packs for the day, which usually included for each of us: a few nuts and seeds, a square portion of tofu, an inch square of goat's cheese and an apple, and then lots of water, of course. Then we grabbed our hats and field glasses for birding and set on our way.

It was an easy hike upstream along the Bash-Bish Brook to the giant 200-foot waterfall. Then we climbed down some steep cobbled steps and sat on a large granite rock, so that we could meditate near the rushing water. All you could hear was the all-encompassing energetic roar of the water as it rushed off of the waterfall cliff. On some days, the sunlight hit at such an angle that it lit up some of the water bubbles that had sprayed onto the rock, making little prisms with a kaleidoscope of color beaming from them. These little prisms looked as if they were little nature spirits that were coming to spy on us and cast magical spells. Perhaps they were sent by the ghosts of Bash-Bish and her daughter, White Swan, who had died in these very special falls, according to Mohican Indian legend.

Bash-Bish[2] was a beautiful Indian woman who had had been accused of adultery by a jealous competitor. The Village Counsel pronounced her guilty and sentenced her to death by being strapped to a canoe and pushed off of the falls. A few minutes before the execution, the sun formed a halo around her body and a ring of butterflies flew around her head, and then the canoe sailed down into the falls. The Indians found the canoe but they never found Bash-Bish's body, which made them believe that Bash-Bish must have been a witch. White Swan, who was Bash-Bish's daughter, was betrothed to Whirling Wind, who was the son of an Indian chief; but when she found that she was unable to conceive a child, she committed suicide by jumping off of the falls. Whirling Wind had been following her that day and he was so shattered by losing her that he also jumped off of the falls. The Indians were able to recover his body, but like her mother, White Swan's body was never found. Therefore, the legend is that the ghosts of Bash-Bish and White Swan live in the Bash-Bish Falls.

Sometimes we took Merlin and Sweetpea with us to the falls. They were contained in their travel carriers during the entire time, but they were able to see the falls and listen to the roaring water. Then we returned to the house to cook our most favorite dinner on the grill, which usually included an appetizer of goat's cheese and crackers, plus grilled salmon with broccoli for the main course, and lots of delicious chardonnay wine.

gh Irene was working with MIT in Boston, Alex, and Kyaaro were still living in the Pepperberg labo- at the University of Arizona at Tucson, until she et up accommodations for them in the Boston area. hile, a breeder gave her a young one-year-old Congo Grey parrot to work with at MIT. The breeder had n able to sell the parrot because he had a handicapped t had been damaged when he was a baby in the nest. feet are very versatile and the way in which they are gives them ease and flexibility in perching and objects, quite similar to a human hand. Specifically, ve four toes with three of them directing forward fourth one directing backwards: this allows them to hings by wrapping the three front toes in one direc- d the fourth toe in the other direction around an In other words, the fourth toe acts similarly to a in the human grasp. All four of the toes on the hand- Grey's left foot directed forward because of the t, and this resulted in his being clumsier than most because he could not grasp perches with the handi- foot. Therefore, since the breeder could not sell the she had kept him with her in her home.

named him Wart, after the legendary King Arthur, as nicknamed Wart by Merlin the Magician when he King Arthur as a child. Wart the Grey was a sweet ergetic little parrot. Irene brought him with her to e girls and me for the weekend, very soon after she ceived him. He was a little shy and unsure of himself e first arrived, but once he felt accepted by Merlin a, his playful personality shone through. I remember

OOPS! I made a silly faux pas! On page 195, I incorrectly stated that parrots' toes (talons) are three forward/one backward. Silly me! I have lectured about the uniqueness of the parrot grip (two toes forward/two backward). This will be corrected in the next printing. Meanwhile, the copy that you have just purchased is special because it will be a "collectors' item." Save it for the grandchildren and ENJOY!!! Maggie Wright cuddling with him over that first weekend to help ease the shyness and confusion that a young parrot usually feels when it first enters a new home situation.

Wart lived in a cage in Irene's office at MIT, where he worked with many of the graduate students, but when Irene had to travel, he came to live with us for a few days at a time. I purchased a new cage for Sweetpea and kept her older one in the house for Wart to live in when he visited. Wart was treated like family, and when we needed to pack up and drive into the city for a few days, he was brought right along with us. Our log cabin home was affectionately called Camp Wright by a few of the MIT students.

My Greys have always slept at night in small carrier cages near my bedroom. This system has really worked well for the girls and me because, not only did it allow me the time to thoroughly cleanse their day cages every night, but the girls could also sleep for longer periods in a dark room, away from the lights and roaring television where their day cages were located. Parrots tend to mess up their cages every day, pooping and dropping food onto the cage bottoms, and sometimes on the floor. In Nature, birds propagate the forest by dropping and throwing around fruits and seeds when they forage; therefore, it is instinct that they tend to be a little sloppy in their cages in human homes. It took me approximately an hour every night to thoroughly clean the cages, but in the long haul, it was really worth it for me to have everything spotless.

When Wart first came to stay with us in the log cabin, I let him sleep at night in the same cage that he was using during the daytime, but that system did not last long. Here's the story! Since the log cabin was not insulated, it obviously had a few holes and openings too, where sometimes the field mice could get in, and there was a little brazen mouse that seemed to know my living room quite well. I had purchased a bag of organic peanuts and had left them in a duffle bag to prepare for our next road trip back to New York City. The little mouse had found the bag of peanuts... and he must have decided that Wart would be a good guard for his new cache. All night long, the mouse took a peanut out of the duffle bag, one at a time, and scrambled across the floor to Wart's cage; he climbed up the cage legs with the peanut in his mouth and stashed it in the corner of the bottom of the cage. This activity must have gone on all night long, and Wart must have watched this mouse climb into his cage, over and over, and over again, because when I went downstairs the next morning for breakfast, I found 47 peanuts all hoarded in a pile in the corner of Wart's cage. I was flabbergasted and did not know whether to laugh or cry! From that moment on, I knew that my system of cleaning up the cages at night so that there would be "NO crumbs left for little critters" was the right idea. I caught the mouse in a Have-A-Heart trap and delivered him to a new forest, approximately 10 miles away from home, because I knew they were smart enough to find their way back into my home, if they were released nearby. Wart's cage was thoroughly cleaned and bleached, and from that day on, he slept at night beside Merlin and Pea in his own small sleeping carrier cage.

In the daytime, Wart and Sweetpea seemed to have contests to see who could play the hardest. The moment I heard lots of screaming (at the toy) and banging of bells, I knew the contest had started. First, there was one bell… and then another bell…then another bell…and another, and so on. This could have been a harrowing experience for someone unfamiliar with parrots because of their loud and raucous screams, which really were screeches of joy.

Wart's visits were great for Irene and me too because we arranged to meet half-way between Boston and Columbia County, New York, at a restaurant off of I-90 for lunch or dinner, while delivering Wart in his travel carrier back and forth. This way, we could see each other more often, and Wart really seemed to enjoy the contrast between his two lives.

MIT released Irene from their contract sooner than expected, due to budget constraints, and so Wart no longer had a home in the MIT office. Instead, he lived full-time with us over a four or five month period, while Irene searched and negotiated a space with Brandeis University, where Wart would then live with Alex and Griffin. It was agreed that Kyaaro (Kyo) would move in with the girls and me on a full-time basis, instead of the new Brandeis Pepperberg Lab, because of the small size of the lab space and the fact that Kyo seemed happier in a quieter environment. The changes would take place at the end of the year.

CONFERENCE JITTERS

"What if we don't get enough interest?" I thought. "What if no one shows up, and I am liable for the expenses?"… "What

if the estimates are wrong and I owe lots of money?" …
"What if the speakers don't show up?" Thoughts…
thoughts… thoughts, and more fears. Whew!

"Calm down, Maggie," I said to myself. "Self, (I sometimes
call myself 'Self') everything is going to be fine! Nothing will
go wrong. NOTHING will go wrong!"

I knew that if I didn't stay centered, and if I focused on
my fears, the spring and summer of 2001 were going to be
long and hot. Besides, Sherrie, the Atlanta Grey Play social
group head and Atlanta conference coordinator, and I were
in constant phone contact and the details leading up to the
conference were in order. So I tried my best not to think too
hard and to have fun.

On Thursday, September 6, 2001, I moved Merlin, Sweetpea
and Wart back into the city with me to prepare for my trip
to Atlanta for the conference, as this would give us a few
days to adjust before I had to take them over to stay with
their sitter in the upper Westside of Manhattan. The birds
were finally settled in at their temporary home on Saturday
and that Sunday, I flew from New York City to Atlanta to
prepare for the conference. Although the speakers and conference attendees were not scheduled to arrive until that
Thursday and Friday, the Atlanta group and I had so much
preparation to do.

On Monday, Sherrie and I met with the hotel staff to go over
every detail of the rooms, the food, the equipment, the audio
visual set-up, the banquet plans, the ballroom set-up, the

break-out room set-ups, and the plans for the Thursday evening "Meet the Speakers" cocktail buffet. Later that afternoon, Lynne, who was responsible for overseeing all of the financials, including attendee payments, met with us to go over all of the details of the finances. That night many other members of the Grey Play group joined us in my master suite to sort out the raffle prizes and to put together the handouts and gifts that had been donated by a few of the advertisers.

Everything was going extremely smoothly, but all that evening of September 10th, I had a feeling of depression and deep gloom. I tried to shake it off, thinking it was just the jitters about the conference. It was almost as if my inner child wanted to run away and hide from something. Why was I so afraid? I had practiced my speeches over and over and over again, ad nauseam, but this sense of fear felt deeper than before. It felt as if something very bad was about to happen, but I could not figure out what it was. I called the sitter in New York City a few times before going to bed to check on my guys, and they were fine. I wanted to cry. What was wrong with me? My gosh, if I was this uptight and depressed on Monday night, how was I going to feel by Thursday night? Sometimes I just did not like being me.

Late that night, I finally got into bed. The lights were out and the room temperature was comfortable, but I couldn't sleep. "Maggie, STOP these stupid fears!" I said to myself. I wanted to cry. I wanted to go home. I wanted to hug my babies, but they were not with me. I tried to focus on beautiful thoughts, such as meditating at Bash-Bish Falls and playing games with the seagulls at Wrightsville Beach. I closed my eyes and imagined my little inner child, whom I called Monty after my childhood name, crawling out of my tummy and cuddling with me, like a little baby. I leaned onto my left side and hugged myself, imagining that I was hugging Monty. "Everything will be okay. Little girl, don't you cry. Everything will be okay," I whispered to my inner child and drifted off to sleep.

"Ring. Ring." I picked up the phone. "Good morning, Ms. Wright. This is your wake-up call from the front desk. It is 7 in the morning."

"Thank you," I said and then hung up. I turned on the television, which I hardly ever watched in the mornings, but this day was different since I was staying in a hotel, and so I tuned to the NBC Today Show. I took a shower and proceeded to get dressed. At approximately 8:30 a.m. the breakfast was delivered to my room, and so I sat down to eat breakfast, read the newspaper, and watch "The Today Show" ALL at one time.

A NEWS BULLETIN came on and it was announced that a small plane had flown into the World Trade Center. They showed the tape of the crash. A few minutes later, a second plane crashed into the second tower, right before my eyes on the television screen! "Oh my God!" I thought. "What's going on!?! This was NO accident," I thought. I immediately picked up the phone and called the pet sitter. I was lucky enough to get through because I had called so quickly after the incidents. I told her to turn on her television set, and she assured me again that she and the birds were all fine and were having a wonderful time… and that she would watch the news. I knew that they were far away from the World Trade Center, so I hung up, confident that they would all be okay.

I was mesmerized and glued to the television set. A few minutes later, Lynne and Sherrie's group came to the suite, and there were NO discussions about the conference. We just sat there, in a daze, horrified at the visuals that were coming before our eyes from the television screen! By this time, the media had announced the Pentagon airplane attack, and they proclaimed that the plane crashes were terrorist attacks and that all airports across the country were being closed down for an unspecified amount of time. Horror upon horror! We then witnessed both World Trade Center buildings collapsing. The day was so horrifying that I can no longer remember the exact sequence of what happened, as it all just seemed to overwhelm us, all at one time.

The telephone rang, and I picked it up. "Hi, I'm Jeff Smart, and I'm supposed to come to your conference. I live a few blocks from the World Trade Center and I can't make it to the conference this week!"

"Hi Jeff," I said. "This is Maggie. Are you okay???"

"I'm okay, but I'm overwhelmed. I'm calling from my cell, and I'm standing out here in the street with soot all over my suit. I don't know what to do next. Gotta go!" he responded in a rushed, despondent voice.

It turned out that Jeff had taken his African Grey to his sister's home on Long Island on that Sunday, so that he could fly out on the following Thursday to our conference. This may have saved the bird's life because she was not stuck in their Battery Park apartment, which again was at ground zero, and as a result, she was saved from breathing all of the toxic smoke flying around Manhattan.

"Ring, ring!" I picked up the telephone again. It was from a friend in New York City who had called to tell me that some of our friends who lived in the WTC area were okay. One particular friend, who groomed my birds and was a bird behavior specialist, had escaped safely from her apartment, which was directly across the street from the WTC south tower.

Gail and her boyfriend, Nat, lived in the 12th floor penthouse apartment of a building that was directly across the street from the WTC south tower. Gail ran a bird sitting business, and so in addition to her own two parrots, there were six other birds staying at her apartment on that morning.

In looking back on that day, Gail described[3] to me a memory of confusion and disbelief. She never really felt fear, but the entire experience was surreal and eerie, everything was different. It was as if she could not think: she was not sure where to go or what to do, but by the grace of God, her boyfriend happened to be home that day, and his incredible wits saved them all.

Gail had just returned to her apartment from voting when the first airplane crashed into the north tower. Fiery cinders and debris were flying everywhere around her building and the air smelled dead and burnt.

Minutes later, there was a fireball explosion, right before her eyes, as the second airplane smashed into the south tower. In living color, in large view from their living room window, they could see the hole where the plane had entered. Heavier debris fell at lightning speed, in pieces and large parts, with the smell of death. Burning cinders poured down onto her building roof, which was right above her apartment. That was when she and Nat decided to put the 8 birds in their travel carriers and then rush downstairs to a friend's 3rd floor apartment.

They placed the birds in a back room that had no windows, while Gail and Nat sat in the kitchen with their two friends who lived with their two dogs in the 3rd floor apartment. They all sat there, numbed, watching the smoke and fire before their eyes and to the backdrop of an indiscernible loud noise...talking through their options.

That was when the south tower building started tumbling down, like a pancake... the 3rd floor apartment kitchen window went black ...and they rushed into the back room with the birds for protection. They were sure this was the end: the collapse was directly across the street.

They knew they had to escape...and they knew that if they did not take the animals, it could be days before authorities would let them back in to get them. But how were they going to carry all 8 birds in their carriers? Their friends had their dogs to contend with. Nat came up with a brilliant solution of wrapping two groups of three carriers together in sheets...and then hanging each group of carriers on either end of a broom pole. Then he soaked the sheets with water to withstand any flying cinders and placed the broom pole across the back of his neck and shoulders, similar to the way in which indigenous farmers carry water. Gail carried the other two carriers, and their two friends were in charge of their dogs.

When they finally left the building, the air was filled with smoke and they could only see a foot ahead of them. Then the north tower tumbled down, and they had to run back into their building lobby for protection. Finally, they left again...four adults, 8 birds in carriers and 2 dogs. They miraculously appeared at another friend's apartment, safe and alive... and their penthouse apartment building happened to be among the very few buildings around the WTC that did not collapse. Another miracle of that day! Amen.

Sherrie, Lynne, and I sat huddled together on the sofa in my hotel suite, watching the horrific day unfold on the television, right before our eyes. It felt surreal. This could not really be happening in New York City... in the United States of America! I tucked my knees to my chest and hugged them with both arms, thankful that I knew my "babies" were okay in Manhattan.

"Sherrie," I said. "We've gotta cancel the conference. This is all too horrifying!"

"I totally agree," she answered. "The airports are closed down. We can't get our speakers here anyway."

Sherrie and I met with the Hilton management that morning to renegotiate for the weekend of November 1, 2001, the only weekend available for the remainder of the year. That afternoon, I contacted all of the conference speakers to notify them that we had canceled the conference and to see if they could attend the weekend of November 1st. It turned out that about a third of them would not be available, so I would need to restructure the conference schedule.

Then, Lynne started calling the conference attendees to notify them of the cancellation of the conference. Most people were accepting of the change; but some were quite furious that we had decided to not have the conference that week. But, we could NOT get the speakers there: there were no airplanes, which meant no speakers, which meant no conference, but STILL some people were upset. The experience was a hassle and a nightmare! In fact, we were being forced by a terrorist attack to have to close down one conference and then re-schedule and re-organize another. In reality, we had to plan two conferences, all in one year.

Now that the conference was cancelled, arrangements had been made for a second one in November, and all attendees and speakers had been notified, it was time to figure out how to get back home to New York City. All airports were closed for the foreseeable future, and who in their right mind wanted to get in an airplane anyway? The only alternative left was to drive, and so Sherrie and I called around to car rental firms to locate a car. We finally found one that would be available in Richmond, Virginia, at noon in two days, which was a LONG way from Atlanta, Georgia. Sherrie offered to drive me to Richmond, an incredibly nice gesture!

On Thursday, we set out on our trip to Richmond, Virginia. Janet, who was one of the conference attendees that had come early for the conference, lived in the Philadelphia area, and so she joined us on the trip, since Philadelphia was on the way and she would be good company for the long drive. We arrived on time in Richmond to pick up the rental car and then proceeded to New York. Later that Friday night, I finally made my way up I-95 to the Newark/New York area.

The night was eerie, and there were very few cars on the highway, which made the atmosphere seem darker than usual, as well as quite spooky and unnerving. As I drove on I-95 parallel to the southern tip of Manhattan Island, I could see the open space where the WTC buildings once stood. The area was lit up by a bright light, similar to how a football stadium appears lit up from a distance, and I could see the bright hue from the lighting and a lot of smoke rising into the night air. "Who would do this to my country?" I thought. "Who could do this to my city?" The next day, I picked up the birds and immediately drove with them back to upstate New York to our log cabin home.

OUR SECOND TRY

The 9/11 experience convinced me that I was NOT going to leave the birds in the city again, while attending the second conference, and so I decided to bring them along to Atlanta with me. Merlin Tewillager got the front seat and Sweetpea and Wart shared the back seat of my old Subaru station wagon that I had named Faith (Old Faithful) because it was so old and had over 200,000 miles on the speedometer. The parrots' carrier cages were chocked full of watery fruits and many vegetables and then toys for chewing. Merle was strapped in the front rider's seat with a sheet covering half of her cage so that she could get in the shade, if the sun started beaming in on the rider's side. Sweetpea and Wart got their own sides of the back seat, and their cages also were half-covered with sheets to protect them from the sun. The radio was turned on full blast, and we had a time, driving down the highway, clicking and clacking, whooping and scream-ing, to whatever boisterous oldie-goldie song that came into play. I truly think road trips are one of the most fun activities for my birds because they are entertained for the entire time.

Two days later, we arrived in Atlanta, ready for the big event. This time, although I was nervous about running my first conference, I felt so much lighter. The conference was smaller with only 100 attendees, which actually was amazing that we had that many brave souls to take the risk of flying to Atlanta, just six weeks after the terrorist attacks. The parrots lived in small cages in my hotel suite, and then they were brought into the conference ballroom during some of the lectures.

Merlin was primed and ready for this event. Actually, given all of the fear and doom and gloom that the media and government had dispersed among the populace following the 9/11 attacks, everyone at the conference seemed ready to feel good and to have a good time. This was a perfect environment for Miss Merlin to show off her "crowd control" skills, giving the right answers... no, the wrong answers... and then asking the crowd to pretend to be a flock of roosters. Although African Greys have a reputation for being intelligent and incredible talkers, extremely few of them are brave enough to make any kind of sounds publicly. This left many in the audience in awe of this little show-off, who was having the time of her life!

Sweetpea and Wart had a wonderful time too! One of the conference attendees brought another African Grey named Heather, who took a "shining" to Mr. Wart, but I'm not sure Wart knew what to do about it.

Speakers, including bird experts Phoebe Linden and Liz Wilson, provided invaluable information and advice to help attendee Grey pet humans better understand their birds. A graduate student Diana May from the Pepperberg Lab showed film of the Congo African Greys in Africa and educated us all about what she had learned about wild Grey behavior when she did field research in equatorial Africa. There were many other incredible speakers, and that Saturday night, we were entertained by the comedy routine of Buckwheat the African Grey and his "straight" pet human, Joe Tyler. The drumming circle group also performed a drumming evening for us during the Saturday evening banquet.

And we heard more miracles that weekend. One of the conference attendees was the regular pilot for one of the hijacked flights, but he happened to take a vacation during the week of September 11th to attend the conference that was canceled. That pilot pet human and his African Grey are now healthy, safe, and ALIVE, today... because of our Camelot 2001 Grey conference that did not happen in September![4]

The weekend was filled with a lot of joy and closeness between a large group of African Grey people, who were thankful to be able to forget their lives for a weekend and to focus on how to better care for these incredible parrots that enrich their lives. The birds and I returned to New York. "Maggie, we done good!" I thought to myself.

LEAVING THE COUNTRY LIFE

It was the end of the year, and I had to let go of my dream of living in the country and move back into the city fulltime, in order to look for a job that could help support me. So in December, we said good-bye to our log cabin and drove away for the final time.

One cold Saturday morning that December, I walked up First Avenue in New York City to get my nails polished. All of a sudden, I looked at the ground and found a little sparrow lying in the middle of the sidewalk. It was an extremely windy day, and the bird had obviously been blown into a window by the horrific wind tunnels that can build in New York City. I picked up the bird and found that it was definitely alive, but quite winded, and so I found a place on the grass to sit that was between some bushes in front of one of the elegant high rise apartment buildings. I cupped my hands and brought the bird to my chest, and then I leaned into the bushes in order to protect it from the wind. I was determined to remain there until it could get its energy back and fly away.

"You're not supposed to be here. Leave now," said a voice. I looked up to see an impeccably dressed doorman wearing his doorman hat and gloves looking down at me.

"Sir, I'm trying to save this bird," I replied and then I lifted my hands to show him the little wee one that was panting to try to get back its breath.

"Ma'am, I don't care what you are doing," he said. "You are not supposed to be here. Leave now."

"Sir, it will only take a few more minutes," I said. "It's so cold out here, and I need a place where I can protect this little bird from the wind."

"Did you hear me?" he retorted. "Do you want me to move you with force?"

"Where is your humanity, sir?" I asked. "I'm not harming your lawn. I'm just trying to help this little bird."

"Lady, it's just a damn bird," he angrily retorted. "Get it out of here, NOW!"

I leaned forward to get up while continuing to hold the little bird cupped in my hands and against my chest, and I slowly walked up First Avenue to find a crevice or deep doorway where I could stand for a few more minutes, to give it a little more time to recuperate. About 15 minutes later, the little sparrow flew up and out, away from my hands.

"Welcome back to New York City, Ms. Wright," I said to myself. I proceeded to get my nails filed and polished, and then I went home to hug my precious little animal companions.

There were many things that I loved about New York City. Most New Yorkers prefer Central Park, but I had a very special place, just off of the East River and four blocks from my apartment, where I loved to go sit. It was my own tiny park area that was located on a concrete embankment that overlooked the East River. It was nothing really special: a line of four park benches and three trees that were off to the right of the benches, but I enjoyed going there as it helped me become centered, when I was upset about something, and even when I was happy.

Every day, I picked up my decaf coffee and cornbread from the Columbus Bakery on First Avenue and then proceeded to my special park that was at the end of East 50th Street. After climbing down steep brick steps, I meandered across a bridge that crossed over a popular dog park and then it crossed over the FDR Drive. Finally, I descended more steps which led to the little park area.

Sometimes, before going to my park, I stood around on the bridge to watch the dogs joyously chase each other around the dog park, while their humans sat on benches, sharing their daily gossip, and some were smoking while others were drinking their water or sodas. The dogs were all sizes and breeds, but they seemed to get along, and they had their special little playmates. A few sat alone with their humans, as perhaps dog-park-time meant having that special alone time with their humans, who probably had busy and hectic lives at home. I wondered. I enjoyed watching the humans and their dogs interact. It made me feel proud of being one of "them," although I did not have a dog companion at the time, because we animal lovers are of the same cloth.

Every day, when I went to my park, my first duty was to hug a special tree, whom I called Sassa, so I guess you can call me a "tree hugger!" I don't even know what kind of tree it was, and it was no larger than 10-12 feet tall, but it represented my symbolic piece of nature in the city, among all of the concrete and gas fumes coming from the cars and trucks on the FDR Drive. Then I sat on a bench to drink my coffee and either read a newspaper or watch the boats go up and down the East River. When the pigeons and seagulls came to visit, I gave them cornbread and talked to them.

In addition to spending lots of time in my little park, I also walked over to St. Patrick's Cathedral on Fifth Avenue, at least two or three times per week, to light candles and pray. Sometimes, I just sat in the beautiful church for a few hours at a time, as it gave me such peace and solace. Although I was an Episcopalian, I found such a spiritual connection with St. Patrick's that I started attending the Catholic services there, instead. My faith helped me to remain calm and know that, no matter how rough things may appear, there is a plan and a path that has been set forward for me.

I missed my country life so much, but I knew I had to be in the city to find a way to support myself. Maybe I could return to the country one day, once my life was more stable. So I pulled out my resume and searched the Internet and the New York Times classifieds for jobs. Week after week, I kept searching...

SWITCHING BIRDS

As Dr. Pepperberg and I had agreed, Wart was going to be returned to Boston to live and work at Brandeis in the new Pepperberg Lab with Alex and Griffin, and Kyaaro (Kyo) would then come to live with me. Irene had compared Kyo, who was a very nervous bird, to a child with attention-deficit disorder, and much of her work with him was being used as the basis for creating educational techniques for teaching autistic human children. I agreed to continue working on his daily sessions with him.

In early January, Diana, a graduate student who had managed the Pepperberg Lab in Tucson, flew Kyo from Tucson to New York City. Even calm parrots can get unnerved when they are out of their territories, and therefore, Kyo, again known for being a very nervous bird, was absolutely terrified when he first came to live with us. He had spent hours all cooped up in his travel carrier while traveling the long distance, completely unsure of what was happening to him, and so when Diana finally opened the carrier in my living room, he immediately jumped out and fluttered around the room. Finally, we were able to get him settled in the cage that had been brought with him; but every time I came near him, he screamed and cowered in the corner of the cage.

I could feel the emotional pain, suffering, and confusion that this little guy was going through. I knew how dedicated I was towards nurturing animals, but Kyo acted so terrified of me that it actually hurt my feelings, at first. Day after day, he continued to cower and scream, as well as flutter in the cage when there was a sudden sound or quick motion that he was not expecting. I let Merlin spend time with him on top of his cage, which seemed to calm him. I also spent a lot of time sitting at a short distance from the cage, just talking to him quietly, in order to slowly build trust between the two of us. I avoided putting my hands in the cage, except to clean it and to give him new foods.

Parrots are prey animals, just like horses, rabbits, cattle, and other birds, and their most powerful emotion is fear. It is normal for parrot companions to become nervous or fearful of certain things, but in some instances, they can become so fearful that they become very nervous, and they can even become so terrified that they revert to phobic behavior.

I wanted to reach in the cage to hug Kyo to let him know that everything would be alright, but I knew that that could send him into an extreme phobic reaction, and so I held back and took it very slowly. I told him how much I loved him;

I gave him a few treats to reward him, when he seemed very calm; and I rubbed his head through the cage bars, when he was calm enough to accept it. And finally, we started his 5-10 minute daily sessions: identifying paper, cardboard, cork, key, and nail. These daily work sessions seemed to provide some focus and structure to help him become more settled and confident in my apartment.

Approximately one week after Kyo had arrived, a graduate student came to pick up Wart to return him to Brandeis. It was not until then that I realized how tight the bond had grown between Wart and me, as I became a basket case, a puddle of water, within minutes after Wart and the student had left. It felt as if I had just lost my mother and Mr. and Mrs. Tewillager the rabbits, all over again.

Once deep loss and grief carve a space in your heart, in your emotional center, that same space gets reignited again, and again, as other similar deep losses happen. I cried over Mother. I cried over Mr. and Mrs. Tewillager. I cried over Tinkerbell…and all of my other lost animals and lost loves. I cried and cried over my loss of Wart. I knew that Wart was really loved by Irene and her student staff, and I was sure that he was really going to be nurtured. It was Wart's destiny to return to work with Dr. Pepperberg, but he will forever be in my heart.

As time passed, Kyo became braver and stronger, and although he continued to be a nervous bird, he loved his head rubs, which he called "tickles," and he regurgitated for me every night, which meant that he loved me.

STRUGGLING TO SURVIVE

We had been back, living permanently in the city for a few months, and finances were extremely low... and to make matters even more difficult, my job search was slowed for a short period because this was the time in January of 2002 when I slipped while carrying the jug of water, crashing my head into the kitchen counter. For weeks and months following the accident, I was sick with blurred vision, nausea, and headaches, and I was forced to sleep for hours at a time during the day to give my body the time to focus on healing. If it were not for the help of my sister-friend Sonia and Mary, an eighty-year-old friend, who occasionally cleaned my apartment and who was dedicated to the birds and me, I do not know how I would have survived. Mary cooked for the birds and me a few times per week, and even though Sonia did not live in the city at the time, she spoke with me on the phone several times every day, giving me ideas for reducing the nausea that were based on her experience from suffering with the Crohn's disease.

I had met Mary in the late 1980s when she was referred to me by a friend. She cleaned my apartment once a month, when I could afford it, but somehow over the time, we became very good friends. She loved to cook for the birds and me because she felt that I was too single and had lost my cooking touch, which was true. Being Southern like me, Mary loved down-home cooking and barbeques, but it was not possible to barbeque in a tiny apartment. Instead, she baked chicken and sautéed a medley of vegetables, combined with cabbage, and then joined me for dinner. Sometimes

I took her out to dinner at a cheap, local diner called the Madison Café that was across the street from my apartment. Although we both were struggling with finances, I wanted to do something for her to show my appreciation for all of her help and cooking.

Mary was single. She had been married twice and her only son lived with his children, her grandchildren, in midtown on the Westside. Mary loved to talk about her grandchildren and her special friend who was twenty years younger than she. Her special friend came over to her apartment every Sunday afternoon, and then in the evenings, he took her out dining and dancing.

Since Mary lived in Harlem, she dressed in ragged and over-sized clothes, so that she would look extremely poor in order to avoid being mugged, even though she was incredibly mentally and emotionally strong for her age of eighty-plus years. She had always dressed in her old clothes without make-up when she came to my apartment, and so it was at first difficult for me to believe that she really had a honey in Harlem. But that realization changed when I invited her to go with me to a Broadway show, many years later in 2007, as a thank-you present for her dedication and loyalty to me and the birds over the years.

"Ring!" my door bell rang, and I opened the door. There was a tall, elegant African American lady standing at my door. She wore a highly styled wig and with impeccable make-up and jewelry adorning her face. She wore a perfectly pressed, spotless designer Ralph Lauren suit that she had probably

found at Goodwill, and her toes were stuffed into long pointed black designer pumps. She carried a long, knotted black
walking cane that was not only a great walking tool, but she
could also use it for defense.

"Wow!" I thought. This was a completely different Mary
than I had ever seen!

"Hello, Miss Wright," she said. I had always asked Mary to
call me Maggie, but she continued to call me "Miss Wright"
anyway.

"Hi, Mary. WOW!" I said. "You are beautiful! Why don't
you dress like this more often?"

"It's not safe, Miss Wright," she answered. "You don't know
what I have to deal with in the area where I live. I'd rather
look poor so no one will mess with me. Did you realize that
one day, someone stole my groceries right out of my hand?
Oh no, Miss Wright, you have no idea."

"Well, Mary," I answered. "You certainly look terrific
tonight!"

We went to see my favorite American Idol, Fantasia Barrino,
perform in Oprah's Broadway Musical "The Color Purple."
The moment that Mary and I got out of the cab, I noticed
eyes following her everywhere, and from that evening on,
I had a completely new image of my dear friend, Mary.

inally in the late spring of 2002, I was able to resume my job search, and I found a consulting job to conduct marketing activities for a small company that sold educational math products for school-aged children. It lasted for almost one year, until they could no longer afford to pay me because they had lost one of their top clients in their telemarketing division that was their primary source of funds for marketing their math products.

So I kept looking and found a few part time jobs here and there, while continuing to focus on the African Grey and animal businesses. My most powerful weapon for withstanding this period of my life was a positive attitude. I believed that I was on the right path, and one day, it would all fall into place.

I created Nature's Corner magazine.

chapter ten

THE ANIMAL RIGHTS PARADOX

I cannot even imagine how things would have turned out had I NOT met my African Grey companions, Merlin Tewillager, Sweetpea and Kyaaro. Life would have gone on, no doubt, and I would have gotten up in the same way in the mornings and had an interesting life, being concerned about the same mundane things as everyone else. But I would have missed out on the beautiful nuances of life... the MAGIC that is all around us; and all we have to do is to look and to become aware of it.

Did you know that we actually do see fairies in our existence? Have you ever sat outside and looked closely at a dragonfly... or at a Monarch butterfly...or at any of the flying insects? The dragonflies have little heads with big eyes and long bodies. They are capable of flying like the hummingbird by moving forward and then hovering in still motion, because they have two sets of wings. As far as I'm concerned, they could be little angels and fairies living right among us.

I don't know that much about insects, and I don't like having them in my home, just like everyone else, but I do prefer to catch them in Kleenex and then let them out of the house, instead of killing them. If there is some sort of infestation, or if there are swarms of them, I have them killed, just like everyone else. However, when I see the individual insect that I can catch alive in a tissue and let out of the house, I will.

One day after a rain storm in the country, I picked up a frog that was in the road and returned him to the nearby pond, so that he would not be run over by a car. The pond was near a busy home construction area, and one of the workmen yelled at me: "Lady, you're just like my wife! My wife… she lets the bugs out of the house. She won't even let me kill them. She's crazy!" That one comment helped me realize that the workman's wife was not crazy, and I'm not crazy. We are among the many animal and nature-loving kindred spirits that live in our communities and neighborhoods, and there are many more of us than we all think.

When I walk around the New York City streets, I find myself periodically looking at the ground to avoid stepping in sidewalk crevices so that I won't twist my ankle or trip. I also look out for other messes, such as food left on the street and the occasional dog poop, even though the "pooper scooper" law has convinced most dog walkers to pick up after their animals' mess. But one day, I was walking along the street in the west 60s, and while looking down I noticed a little bug struggling. Please believe me that I do not usually put my hands anywhere near the ground of the dirty streets, but this day, and for some reason, something made me stop and put my finger beside the struggling bug. A magnificent dragonfly then grabbed onto my finger and as I pulled up my hand, it flew off.

Apparently, dragonflies can get caught up in the New York City (or any big city) wind tunnel drafts, just like other flying creatures, and when they are knocked over onto their backs, they cannot right themselves. Instead, they are stuck, lying on their backs on the sidewalk, and helplessly awaiting the fate of being stepped on and smashed by some busily walking New Yorker.

I stood there for a moment… amazed. I had just saved the life of a little creature. As the Universe sends people and circumstances our way to help us in troubled times, I thought I must have been sent by the same big Universe to save this little creature.

In looking back on the past decade of my life, I find that when I have been upset about something, or even nervous about something, I always turned to Mother Nature and her animals. I hung out with my guys and played with them; or I sought solace by communing with my tree Sassa by the New York City East River; or I meditated beside the Bash-Bish waterfalls in western Massachusetts; or I hung out with the seagulls at the beach; or I relaxed in my backyard with the chipmunks, squirrels, birds and other critters. It's not just because of the calming effect, and it is not just because of the MAGIC, but it's also because Nature is our home too. We humans are just another creature of Nature and I am coming home!

We, as a species, have become separated from our roots, and our technology-based society, in addition to all of the fear campaigns of this and that disease, have put up a wall to separate us from Nature. Our children and grandchildren have no idea what it is like to hide in the woods to watch the animals... or to get filthy dirty while playing in the mud; but instead, they live their virtual reality lives playing with their computer games. Even if they were 'kicked outside' and forced to play, most of them would have no idea how to use their imagination and to open to the magic. But it is never too late.

Our family dogs, cats, and other animal companions represent the closest connection that many of us have ever had with nature, especially over the past few decades. I believe that our animal companions are in our lives to awaken us and to guide us back. They have been so patient and accepting of us, in spite of our misperceptions that they were nothing more than mere automatons; but finally, many of us are coming around and realizing how intelligent they really are.

I created a new magazine called *Nature's Corner*® magazine whose objective was to educate the world of animal lovers about the intelligence and sentience of their animal companions and other critters of Nature. It was an evolutionary restaging of my African Grey magazine, and I created it by becoming my own marketing consultant. After over a decade of struggling to build the *Grey Play Round Table*® African Grey magazine, I finally decided to put on my marketing cap and to figure out how to restage it into something that may have a broader appeal. I had not been able to build the Grey magazine's circulation over 1500 to 2000 subscribers, even though it had garnered a good reputation for putting out cutting edge information to help Grey owners better understand how to work with their parrots. One problem was that people did not seem to want to pay for the information because they believed they could get it for free over the Internet. Instead, many of them became even more confused, given the conflicting and erroneous advice that was in articles and email groups all over the Net. Secondly, Jane Hallander and Alicia McWatters, who were two of my key writers that had worked with me from the inception of the magazine to build its cutting edge reputation, had died. This basically demolished the proposition for the magazine; therefore, it was time for a serious restaging.

I treated the magazine business like a mature branded product, as I would have in the corporate packaged goods marketing world. I brainstormed and meditated over how the African Grey parrot is perceived in the world of Grey owners and non-owners, exactly as I would have studied the ice cream market, for example.

Finally in 2005, the AH-Ha! came to me. African Greys were perceived by owners and non-owners to be extremely intelligent animals, and animal cognition science was proving that many other animals were also highly intelligent thinking/feeling creatures; therefore, the new magazine could reach a broader base by exploring intelligence and sentience of all animals. So I researched the animal and science magazine businesses to see how they positioned their magazines, and I found that none of them really focused on this specific area. There were lots of dog, cat, bird, and other animal magazines that focused on the regular care of the pets, as well as science magazines that focused on the environment. There were others that emphasized feeding backyard birds and landscaping the backyard, and finally, there were some that focused on specific issues, such as holistic health for animal companions. But still, none of them did what I wanted to do.

There were many terrific magazines, such as *Science, Nature, and Seed,* which touched on animal intelligence, but their target seemed to be comprised of the more intellectually oriented environmental types of people. I wanted to create a mass magazine for the ordinary animal lover like me, a sort of high quality *People* that explored animal intelligence and sentience.

I created a business proposition and then named the new magazine *Nature's Corner*®. My graphics designer friend Chris and I worked on a new design. Since I had overseen 100s of focus groups in my packaged goods marketing career and had been through moderator training with the RIVA Institute, I decided to run my own focus groups about the concept. I spoke with middle income pet-loving women who had subscribed to animal magazines within the past few years, and they were extremely excited about the idea.

Within a few months time, we put up a website for the magazine and I hired Sue, a very talented professional, to help me with the search engines and to manage a new BLOG. I also found a few good writers and we put together our first issue. I hired a young professional lady named Maria, who had worked in the Pepperberg Lab and was planning to pursue her Ph.D. in animal science, to write some of the lead science articles.

Everything was set and ready to go for our first issue. We printed 5000 copies and sent them to old subscribers of my former African Grey magazine, in addition to a direct mail animal lovers list. I advertised in magazines that held our target audience, such as *Bird Talk*, *Hobby Farms*, *Wild Bird*, and *Animal Wellness*, in addition to a few regional animal oriented newspaper magazines.

I was SO excited about the potential for this little magazine. Other professionals with whom I had spoken seemed to think it was going to be very successful too, but unfortunately, we got very few subscribers. What happened? Where did I go wrong? Focus group members had LOVED the concept of the magazine, but no one was buying it.

I realized that magazines were extremely difficult to market. Most new magazine marketers followed the selling strategy of sending out free copies of their issues, until consumers eventually started subscribing, but I was a little entrepreneur without deep financial pockets, so I could not afford to keep sending out free issues ad infinitum. Therefore, I decided to publish a second issue in 2006 and then to take a hiatus to further research this magazine business opportunity and to figure out where I had gone wrong.

In late 2006 and 2007, I conducted more focus groups, but

this time, I was able to show them copies of our new magazine. Specifically, I showed them copies of competitive magazines, in addition to copies of *Nature's Corner*, and asked them for their likes and dislikes and how they would compare our new magazine to the others. I was amazed how 'into these magazines' these consumers were. They gave their opinions about font sizes, column layout, and spacing between lines, which shocked me. There was a certain way in which publications had to look or they would not be considered to be good magazines, according to the consumers. Not only that, they told me, through a lot of in-depth probing on my part, exactly how the magazine must speak to them, if I wanted it to become successful.

Positioning this new magazine was becoming as difficult as positioning light beer, for example. Light beer was originally marketed as a diet beer for diet-conscious consumers, but it was never successful until the Phillip Morris Corporation (owners of Miller Beer) did a brilliant advertising positioning job to make it acceptable to the regular beer drinking consumers. It was developed in the 1960s under Piel's Trommer's Red Label brand in 1961, and then as Rheinghold's Gablinger Diet Beer in 1967. In the mid to late sixties, Meister Brau marketed it as a "lite" beer that was "lighter and less filling," but the company ran into financial troubles and the lite brand was sold to Phillip Morris' Miller Brewing business.

Miller marketing executives discovered that the Meister Brau lite product sold well in a few blue-collar markets, which suggested that it had potential for appealing to regular beer-drinking consumers. Therefore, they reformulated the product and then researched and tested it against Coors Beer, which was a milder and lower calorie beer. In 1975, Miller introduced Miller Lite Beer and positioned it as a "great tasting, less filling beer that you could drink more of in one sitting." This new positioning combined with the masculine pro-sports and macho images in the advertising made the brand a major success.

In short, Miller took a product that was not succeeding and restaged it so that it appealed to their target audience. This was to be my challenge for building the *Nature's Corner*® Magazine business.[1]

In 2008, Peter and Duane, two magazine industry professionals, helped me put together the Alex Memorial issue by incorporating the consumer changes. Then, I placed the magazine "on hold" until I could find the right team to help me build it.

HUMANE TREATMENT

I wanted to create *Nature's Corner* Magazine because of my deep love and reverence for all of Nature, including all companion animals and other critters of nature. It is our spiritual and physical responsibility to ensure that they are respected; and I believe that all animals, whether they are pets, wild animals, livestock, or laboratory animals, have the right to be treated humanely. I wish for them to live out their lives with minimal suffering, fear, hunger, and pain.

I do not believe in any form of hunting or fishing for sport or trophy, although I am not completely innocent of this act. I grew up in a family of hunters, and I enjoyed fishing with my brother and father during much of my life; but for some reason, I did not think about the negative aspects of hunting and fishing, until my life was changed by living with my parrots.

I remember the first day of deer hunting season when my birds and I first moved to the country in Upstate New York. I was driving down a quiet two-lane country highway. The day was chilled, but the sun was shining bright, and I was on the way to the grocery store. All of a sudden, a large herd of deer rushed across the highway and I smashed my foot onto the brakes, thankfully missing them. As the deer crossed to the other side, they seemed stressed and agitated, and they seemed confused, as if they did not know where to go next. A few members of the herd ran to the left, stopped and then turned to follow the others as they disappeared into the forest. I pulled my car off to the side of the road and sat there for a few minutes; I had to process a mixture of feelings going through me. First, I was so saddened to witness the stress and fear that they seemed to be going through: how horrible it must feel to know that you are being stalked to be killed. My body was weak and my legs were shaking because of the stark realization that had the deer run across the road, just five seconds earlier, it may have been too late to step onto the brakes. Memories of this harrowing day stick heavily in my mind.

One of our neighbors was a prolific hunter. He dressed himself up in what appeared to me to be an army camouflage outfit, topped off by a tan wide-brimmed ranger hat that was folded and pinned on one side by an eagle's feather that was stuck in the side. He got onto his little amphibian jeep, carrying along multiple shot guns. He looked to me like he was going off to war, to kill some defenseless deer so that he could put its head or antlers on his wall. As I watched him go off to war, I prayed for the little deer that was going to be killed that day, and for its buddies and family that were going to lose him.

Although I am against hunting, I do not hold a grudge against hunters. There are many hunters who say they love animals and Nature as much as I do, but their perspectives are different. Many believe they are actually caring for the animals by controlling their populations and they are contributors to conservation efforts. I am not here to judge the hearts of others, but I can pray that through some life experience, their perspectives may change, as mine did.

But there is one area that I cannot tolerate: any form of live animal shoots or animal fighting, such as dog and cock-fighting. In these illegal situations, animals are not given even the slightest chance of escape or survival. For example, Pennsylvania is the last state to allow live pigeon shoots. Hunting clubs release tame pigeons from cages so that their members, who are no further than 60 feet away, can shoot them for target practice. Most of the birds do not die right away, and so the organizations allow young children between the ages of 8 and 14 years old to wring the birds' necks or kick and slam them onto the ground to kill them before throwing their carcasses into sacks. These children are called "trapper boys." At this writing, there is pending legislation in the Pennsylvania Legislature to ban live pigeon shoots. I hope that this time, it is approved.[2]

There is nothing "hunting" about these cruel, horrific, live-animal killings. Responsible hunters who say they love Nature would practice their hunting skills with clay pigeons, not real, alive pigeons. Clay pigeons are clay targets that are released from a trap to simulate the flight of a bird so that the hunter can practice his bird-shooting skills. When I was a teenager, Daddy used to take me along on his clay pigeon shoots, which he called skeet shooting. Daddy tried to teach me how to shoot a shotgun, but my biggest memory from this experience was my sore shoulder that got constantly bruised by the kickback power of the shotgun.

I also am opposed to pets that kill-for-sport. To me, a well-fed companion dog or cat that prowls on backyard small animals, birds and their fledglings is doing it for sport, although I hear the argument that it is their right: they are acting on their instinct to kill. Humans had an "instinct" to kill too, when they were cavemen; but as civilized citizens of planet Earth, this instinct has been curbed. Similarly, cats can be responsibly trained not to attack innocent wildlife. According to many Internet sites that I've read, approximately 65% of cat owners let their cats roam their neighborhoods. These sites also claim that outdoor cats are responsible for the killing of large numbers of birds, small mammals, reptiles, and amphibians. Most birds and other animals that are attacked by cats will most likely die because of the toxic bacterium, which is found in cats' claws and teeth.

There was a neighborhood cat that enjoyed stalking and killing the doves that fed in the backyard of one of my homes. He would hide behind a bush and then pounce on an innocent dove, mangle it a little, and then leave it to die in my backyard. I constantly tried to scare and chase the cat from my yard, and finally, I started getting up at 5 a.m. every morning, so that I could scout out my backyard and chase the cat away before the birds came to feed. Finally, the cat stopped coming to the yard.

Owners who believe their cats have a right to roam freely must realize that many of their neighbors do not want these cats roaming through their yards; so be a good citizen and curtail your cat before someone creates a new law to do it for you. There are commercial fences that cats cannot climb over or under that would allow them to continue to freely roam, but only in their owners' backyards.

My friend Jerry kept his two cats in his home at all times because he was concerned about the birds in his backyard. Actually, there was a grackle that came for many years to visit Jerry and his cats. It perched on the same tree limb for approximately 30 minutes every day, and Jerry was convinced that the bird was a friend of Allie, one of his cats, because Allie always appeared so calmly attentive at the window when the bird came around, as if they were communicating.

More and more animal control laws are popping up across communities because of one or two incidents of pet attacks on other animals, children, or neighbors. The pit bull is the first that comes to mind, and unfortunately, the entire pit bull breed is facing a bad reputation, because of the few "bad apple" dogs that were not properly trained and/or housed. It was not the dogs' fault for attacking other animals, children, or neighbors, but in most cases, it was the problem of their humans who did not take the responsibility to train or properly house them. Most pit bulls are wonderful dogs, but they get maligned and more legally controlled because of the bad antics of the few; and the more laws that are created on the books, the less freedom we have as animal owners to care for our companions. Therefore, we need to take the responsibility first, and ensure that our animals, including our cats, dogs, birds, horses, rabbits, and so on, are good "neighborhood citizens," and then there will be no need for any more legal intervention.

Again, I believe that animals have the right to be treated humanely, but I learned the hard way that my definition of "right" is different from that of the Animal Rights organizations. Here is what happened:

When we created the *Nature's Corner* Magazine website, I searched the Internet for emotional photographs of animals of different species getting along and loving each other. Finally, I found some on a website, and I got permission from that website's organization to use the photographs in a revolving animal photo format on our site. Then I got permission from Jim Jenkins to use his beautiful "Because I Love You So" instrumental as background music for those viewers that wanted to hear sound. The combination of the loving photos and emotionally compelling musical background gave me the shivers. At times, I loved to close my eyes and sway and float in spiraling circles all around my home office to the beautiful music, as it blasted from my computer. I was so excited about the prospects of this new magazine, as well as about what it could do to help educate the world about animal intelligence and sentience.

"Dear Maggie, I noticed that your new site does advertising for Animal Rights organizations. If that is true, I will NEVER subscribe to your magazine." Within days of opening my new *Nature's Corner* website, I received this email.

"What?" I thought. "What's going on?"

"Dear Janet," I wrote back. "You have been associated with me and my writing for over 11 years, and you know I have had nothing to do with the Animal Rights type of organizations."

Janet wrote back. "A friend of mine noticed that an Animal Rights organization is advertising with you. If you are associated with them, I cannot participate with your magazine. The Animal Rights issue is a big area of concern for serious pet animal lovers."

It turned out that the organization from whom I had gotten the loving animal photos was an Animal Rights group, and I had put up a cyber-link to their site, as a way of saying thank you for the use of the photos. Well, within one day, the cyber-link was deleted and the photos were replaced.

I remember being very confused for a while. Why were animal lovers so adamantly opposed to the "Animal Rights" movement? Of course, I understood why most animal people disassociated themselves from the animal liberation extremists that burned homes and threw paint onto fur coats as protests, but it took me a while to understand why they wanted nothing to do with anything related to the general movement of rights. Finally, it became obvious to me that there were two major platforms for animals: animal welfare and animal rights.

ANIMAL WELFARE (AW) is the perspective that animals must be respected and given a decent life. Humans have a moral responsibility not to cause animals to suffer excessively. In other words, this perspective argues that it is okay to use animals in certain ways, such as for food, but it is our obligation to assure them a humane life and a death with the least amount of suffering.

ANIMAL RIGHTS (AR) is the perspective that animals, or at least certain animals, have the right to possess their own lives. They should not be used in any form by humans, such as for food or for clothing, and they should suffer absolutely no pain or suffering.

One of the key differences between the two perspectives boils down to the issue of 'animal use.' The AR viewpoint does not believe animals should be used for anything, including pet ownership, and they want to abolish all animal uses, including pet ownership. One of the first steps on the path to annihilate pet ownership is to change the terminology and legal status of animals. Right now, animals are considered to be our personal property, but many of the activists want to change it so that we are their "guardians," instead of their "owners." They argue that animals should not be legally designated as property or things that can be treated as the owner sees fit. Their premise is that the touchy-feely term of pet guardianship "promotes a more compassionate relationship between person and animal,[3]" and it more closely reflects the bond that is between humans and their animal companions. But what does it really do?

Again, our pets are our private property. That means that under the United States Constitution our private property pets cannot be taken away from us without a search warrant, and we have the right to defend our property rights in public court with Due Process of Law. However, "Guardianship" could restrict our rights as pet owners.

According to attorney Genny Wall, 2005 Avian Welfare Chair for the American Federation of Aviculture, we will no longer own our pets if our legal status is changed to "Guardians," rather than "Owners" of our pets; but instead, the government will own them. She says, "In legal terms, the rights and obligations of a 'Guardian,' and the Guardian's abilities to resist intrusion from outsiders, are limited when compared to the rights and abilities of an 'Owner.' A person who owns property has rights under the U.S. Constitution not to be deprived of that property without Due Process of Law. In contrast, a 'Guardian' does not enjoy the same level of Constitutional protections afforded to an 'Owner.'... Due Process can require a much higher standard of proof and more structured and stringent legal procedures to remove an animal from an 'Owner' than from a 'Guardian.' A 'Guardian' can be easily and quickly appointed, and just as easily and quickly removed, by a judge, often without a hearing or trial.... If we are 'Guardians' rather than owners, then ultimately it will be the State, and not the individual, who has the power to say who will care for the animal, how it will be cared for, where it will reside, what medical treatments it will or will not undergo, and who will make all the other decisions regarding the health, welfare, life and death, or destruction of that animal.[4]"

Some guardianship supporters try to make the concepts of "ownership" and "property" look bad by making us feel that if we see our animals as property, then we must not care about them as beings or creatures, and we do not see their lives as mere animals to be valuable. This is a lie.

Even while being legally designated as property, animals have ethical protection from abuse under the law. In a position paper entitled, "Animals Are Not Things," Dr. Temple Grandin, renowned animal welfare and livestock handling expert, postulates that even though animals may be legally considered to be property, they have more legal protection from unethical abuse than other things that may be property. She uses the comparison of a cow to a screwdriver, which are both property. To paraphrase, she states that you can chew up, destroy, or mangle a screwdriver, but there are legal restrictions on what can be done to the cow.[5]

Of course, there always needs to be more responsibly

written legislation that protects the welfare of animals, which I would wholeheartedly support. However, animal ownership is a completely different subject from animal welfare, and the legal change in animal status would contribute nothing towards animals having better lives. To the contrary, it could separate them from the ones who truly love them and want to protect them: their owners.

Since the 1970s, the area of "Animal Rights" has grown from being a fringe idea with a few outspoken supporters to a powerful, sophisticated law-based movement. According to Richard L. Cupp, Associate Dean for Research at Pepperdine University Law School, approximately 70 U.S. law schools have added animal law studies, which include both animal welfare and animal rights directions (Wikipedia has estimated that 97 out of 180 U.S. law schools offer animal law). Further, Bob Barker, former Price is Right TV host, has gifted nine top law schools with million-dollar endowments to build animal rights centers.[6] In other words, this is a big movement that is not going to disappear any time soon. Over the coming years, the multitude of animal law graduates may fill strategic spots, such as judgeships and political positions on the local, state, and national levels, in addition to legal jobs, which could make this movement even more difficult for us animal owners to withstand. That is why we animal owners need to come together now.

Associate Dean Cupp, who has written extensively on animal versus human rights, says, "The holy grail for many animal rights activists is abolishing animals' property status."[6] One of their many strategies has been to change the status through local, state, and federal laws. At this writing, fifteen cities and localities in the United States and the entire state of Rhode Island have already incorporated local ordinances to change animal ownership language to that of guardianship.[7] I sincerely hope the citizens of these communities are fully aware of the implications of what their elected officials have done.

There also have been numerous legislative attempts to change animal ownership status. One example of anti-animal- ownership legislation was West Virginia's SB277 bill, called the West Virginia Animal Regulation Act, which almost passed in 2005. This bill would have defined many pet species as "exotic animals," such as any pet birds, fish, reptiles, and other small animals; and it would have prohibited their ownership without a special permit to possess them. Had it passed, the bill would have eliminated pet ownership for these animals as property under the U.S. Constitution. On top of that, it would have given authority to the newly created Exotic Animal Regulation Board to search, seize, quarantine, and destroy any 'exotic' animal, if "THEY" determined it to be harmful to 'other people, plants or wildlife;' and human companions of these animals would have had absolutely no legal recourse for protecting them from being taken away from their homes by the State. The West Virginia SB 277 bill had already unanimously passed the State Senate and was headed for the House, but thankfully, animal owners and lovers from all over the country caused such an uproar that the bill died.[8] Dog owners, cat owners, bird owners, reptile owners, rabbit owners, and many, many more animal owners and lovers banned together, and the West Virginian legislators received nonstop phone calls, emails, and letters from 8 to 5 on the days of the hearings. This was a significant accomplishment because had the bill passed, it would have jeopardized the welfare of many pets in West Virginia. Not only that, it would have set a precedent for other state legislatures across the country to follow.[9]

ANIMALS AS LEGAL PERSONS

Many AR activists intend to pursue personhood and basic liberty and equality rights, which they call "dignity-rights,"[10] for some intelligent animals, such as chimpanzees and gorillas, based on these animals' intellectual abilities and the fact that they are so much like humans. This does not mean that the animals would have all of the rights that are given to humans, such as the ability to go to school and vote, but it means that they would have basic human rights, such as the right to life, freedom from arbitrary captivity, and protection from torture. The goal of the activists is to get one state court to agree, which would then set a legal precedent for other states to follow.[12] Following along with this flow, precedent would then be set to pursue dignity-rights for other intelligent animals, such as dolphins and African Grey parrots, and possibly eventually dogs, and so on. We would no longer be considered "owners" of our African Grey pet companions, and even of our dogs, if they were given dignity-rights.

In Austria, there is a case before the European Court of Human Rights to declare a 28-year-old chimp named

Matthew to be a "person," so that he can have a legal guardian and his own funds for being cared for.[11] AR activists claim that they are not trying to send Matthew to school, but they are fighting for "his basic right not to be killed." He currently lives in a Vienna-based shelter that is going bankrupt and the chimp supporters want their financial support for Matthew to go directly to him, instead of the shelter. By Austrian law, only humans can receive monetary gifts and have guardians.[12] If Matthew's personhood is approved, it will set a legal precedent across Europe that apes should be treated with many of the same rights as people. They would no longer be legally considered to be property. If AR activists really love animals, as they claim they do, I do not understand why they do not set up a fundraising effort to help the entire facility and to save ALL of the animals in the facility, in addition to Matthew. It is my personal point of view that they should pursue "basic protection rights" through well-thought-through animal welfare laws, instead of personhood.

I believe that giving animals the same basic rights as humans, including just the dignity-rights, sets up a very dangerous game, as well as too many far-reaching implications. If the AR movement is successful at convincing courts to grant personhood to intelligent animals, what's next? Robot pets? Humanoid robots? Even professionals in the field of artificial intelligence are expressing their concerns and fears about our future with robots. In her article, "Robots: Our Helpers or Replacements?" Laura Lorek of *Interactive Week* says, "the idea of a fully automated and intelligent robot has many technology futurists worried about the dangers robots may pose to humans."[13] Further, in the same article, she writes: "Ray Kurzweil, a pioneer in the field of artificial intelligence, sees a future in which humans and robots are so alike it's difficult to tell them apart. Within 20 years, he says, computers will not just be intelligent, they will be conscious, feeling beings deserving of the same rights, privileges and consideration people give each other."[14] I believe that once you walk down the path of giving personhood to any animals, it sets a precedent for scary future scenarios, and the souls who open that original door to this path will be ultimately and eternally responsible.

No NAIS

Most of us eat meat in some form, although a few people have chosen vegetarian diets over meat-eating because of their concern about the animals. I am similar to those who feel okay about eating fish, chicken, or hamburger, as long as the animal was treated humanely. I've never actually tried to cut out all meat and dairy from my diet, although I've dramatically cut down the amount of meat-eating. I eat organic foods whenever possible, and I always look for products whose companies seem to respect the animals and give them a quality of life. For example, I will only purchase eggs from free-range hens that are fed 100% organic vegetarian diets.

I cringe when I read about the horrid conditions in which some farm animals are forced to live. For that reason, I am a great admirer of the work of animal welfare expert Dr. Temple Grandin of Colorado State University, who spearheaded reform in the quality of life of agricultural animals. Temple Grandin is autistic and she discovered that she had much in common with animals because they both think visually. As a result of thinking similarly to animals, she is able to visualize environments from the perspective of an animal, thereby detecting situations and objects that may frighten them. She helps agricultural farmers better understand how to set up their farms so that the animals are humanely handled. Accordingly, her recommendations have helped meat packers comply with the Humane Slaughter Act, as well as to improve the lives of their herds while they are still living.[15]

Although we pet owners and animal lovers may seem to be diametrically opposite to animal agricultural farmers, we actually share common ground with them. Like us, these farmers are facing legislative battles where 'ownership' of their farm animals is being challenged. Specifically, the USDA has created an animal tracking program that they call the "National Animal Identification System" (NAIS), which if implemented, it will not only deprive farmers of their property rights, but it will also invade personal privacy.

According to the NAIS program, a "farmer" is anyone who owns ONE horse, cow, pig, sheep, deer, elk, bison, chicken, and other birds, such as pigeons, and other livestock animals. That means that anyone that has a pet horse, pigeon, chicken, or pig would be forced to comply, and with just the stroke of a pen, other animal pets could be included in the program overnight.[16]

The stated purpose of NAIS is to track livestock animals in order to identify their locations within 48 hours for disease containment. That means if there is a breakout of Mad Cow disease, for example, this program should help identify the source of the sick cow within two days.[17] How wonderful! The government wants to protect us, but let's look deeper at the devil in the details of the proposed program.

If this program is passed, it means that EVERY PERSON that owns even one horse, cow, pig, chicken, sheep, deer, elk, bison, other birds, such as pigeons, and other livestock animals, will be forced to register their home information into a government database, which includes that owner's name, address, and telephone number. EVERY ANIMAL on that premises will be assigned a 15-digit ID number by the government. The ID will be in the form of either a tag or a microchip that contains a radio frequency so that the government can track every single movement of that individual animal by satellite. NAIS would empower a federal agent to enter private premises and seize property, meaning any tracked animal, without a warrant.[18]

Not only that, the owner of the individual animal will be required to report within a 24 hour period any movement of the animal that is off of the premises. For example, if a person decides to ride their horse down the street to visit a neighbor, or decides to take a trail ride that is off the premises, the government must be informed within 24 hours.

There was such an uproar about this program that the Bush administration decided to make it only voluntary; BUT and instead, they have encouraged individual states to legislate mandatory compliance to the NAIS program. Therefore, do not let this fool you!

Opponents of the program believe that it would prove to be so costly and time-consuming that the small farm and local sources of organic food production businesses would dry up, leaving way for the large corporate agribusinesses to completely control what we eat, how it is treated, and how it is produced, whether or not we want to eat genetically-altered foods.[19] And the battle to protect our animals and private property continues ...

THE POWER OF ONE VOICE

We are in serious danger of losing control over what happens to our beloved pets; however, if we animal-loving citizen-owners join hands across animal species and breeds, we will form an impenetrable wall that can and will protect our feathered and furred friends. Education is our first level of defense, so I ask you to please do your own homework on these issues. In the back of this book in the "reference and footnote" section, I have compiled a listing of a few of the Internet websites that discuss the pet ownership versus guardianship issues. Look beyond the "myths." Look beyond the rhetoric that the word "property" is BAD because it is not. Look beyond the sound bytes on the websites that have touchy-feely, pretty words to make us believe they are doing 'good' for animals, and observe what is really happening.

Standing up for our critter pets and companions is one of the most important things we can do for them, because they cannot do it for themselves. We must become more political and we must show up in force to protect our rights as owners. If the AR activists are successful at ending animal ownership, they would succeed at widening the gap between humans and Nature, and the "We" versus "Them" schism would deepen further. I shudder at the thought of not having my parrots in my life, my animal companions who have completely changed the way in which I view life. Most of the Animal Rights extremists are probably not very different from me, having had difficult life experiences and thereby transferring their self-compassion to the animals. Some have probably had even more difficult lives than mine, but the difference here is perspective.

Animals do not see themselves as property and they do not see themselves as little persons either, with all kinds of legal rights. They just love us and they want to be in our lives to teach us, to guide us, and to reconnect us with Nature. I do not see my animals as objects that I can do with as I please, but for their sakes, I will fight for the right to keep them legally classified as 'property' under the United States Constitution. As long as we animal lovers and owners reach across unfamiliar territories, uniting with other animal lovers: pet owners, hunters and farmers with integrity, environmentalists, scientists, nothing can stop us. WE THE PEOPLE can do wonders. Just think of the possibilities!

Merlin was my feathered partner.

chapter eleven

I LOVE YOU SO HARD!

ing! Ring! Ring!" My telephone rang at 6:30 a.m. in my Phoenix, Arizona home.

"Darn it," I thought. "Who is calling me this early ... those darned telemarketers?" Usually when someone called me THAT early in the morning, it was a telemarketer calling my New York telephone line that was call forwarded to Arizona. "I won't pick up," I thought. I grabbed the bed covers and pulled them over my head to get a few more minutes of sleep. It was Friday morning, September 7, 2007, and I had stayed up very late the night before working on my book. I needed a little more time to sleep.

"Ring! Ring! Ring!" It rang again at 6:40 a.m. "That's weird," I thought. "Is there an emergency? Maybe someone really is trying to reach me. Who in the world would call this early in the morning? Thank God all of my babies are here and all is fine. Better get it."

The caller ID monitor was on the kitchen telephone, so with

one eye open, I reached for my bedroom slippers and bathrobe, and then I clumsily rushed down the hallway to the kitchen. The message light was blinking, and so I punched it to listen to the message.

"Maggie, it's Irene. I lost Alex! He died! He died in his sleep last night! What am I going to do? Please call me!!!"

"WHAT?" It was my dear friend Irene Pepperberg in the most distraught and tearful voice I had ever heard. "Oh, my God! NO! Not Alex!" I thought. I immediately called her back.

Irene needed the time to mourn privately, and so I suggested that she not make a public announcement about his death until Monday. She was emotionally devastated; she had lost her baby...her best friend... her colleague. Her entire life had been dedicated to Alex, and everything else was treated as second priority. Every moment she had... and every penny that she had made went to "their" scientific work. Sometimes she pushed off purchasing new business suits and shoes so that the monies that she made could go to Alex, and she kept her furnace thermostat very low at 57 degrees in her Massachusetts home during the freezing winters, just to save money for the Alex Foundation. Her dedication and love for that bird and his junior colleagues never stopped; it never wavered. And now, he is gone.

Stunned, I got dressed haphazardly. I just pulled something out of the closet, not even aware if anything matched, as it didn't seem to matter. Normally, I would get the birds up with me and let them play on their playpens while I prepared their morning veggies," but this morning, I left them in their sleeping cages while I fumbled through the refrigerator to prepare their food.

I walked into the room where they slept at night. "Merlin, Alex is gone!" I cried. My body shook and my chest jerked, as I could feel the emotion and tears well up in my heart. "Kyo, your friend Alex is gone! Sweetpea, our Alex is gone!" I don't know if they understood about Alex being gone since they did not see him on a daily basis, but they seemed to know that something very sorrowful had just happened. I placed each bird in his day cage, one at a time, and left the room. There was silence... they did not make a sound all morning long.

I sat down at my computer to work on my book, but the words would not come through very easily. Every 30 minutes, I checked my e-mail: my social connection with the rest of the world. Then the Alex e-mails started; Alex's death was too big to be kept secret over the weekend. As each e-mail announcement was cross-posted over and over again, I cried harder.

Early that afternoon, I brought Merlin out of her cage to hang out on her playpen that was in my office/living room while I attempted to work on my computer. It was too hard to concentrate, as I was just too sad. How could Alex die? He was larger than everything else. He was not supposed to leave us! I found myself working for a few minutes, and then hugging myself and crying for another few minutes.

"I love you so hard!" Merlin proclaimed to me as she perched on her playpen. "It's ALL that matters."

"WHAT?" I thought to myself. "How did Merlin know to say that?" When she was a young chick, I had taught her to say, "I love you so much!" But as she got older, her love had deepened for me, and so she changed the phrase on her own to say, "I love you so hard." "So hard" meant that she loved me deeper than before, and it makes sense. It is as if saying, "I love you harder [than before.]" But this is coming from the mind and the beak of an African Grey parrot... not a human person.

Then to top things off, she had added "It's all that matters." How did she know that? She had never spoken that phrase before that day, and I had never tried to teach her to say it. I rushed over to the playpen and hugged her. "Merlin," I said. "I love YOU so hard too!"

As the week of September 10th started, the news of Alex's death spread like a wildfire, and with each passing day, the story got bigger and bigger. A *New York Times* Internet article on Alex became the TOP story and the most "clicked on" article of the week. His death also made the big network news programs, as well as CNN, *Time*, and *People* magazines. His story seemed larger than the 9/11 terrorist anniversary, as well as the deaths of Luciano Pavarotti and Jane Wyman; and the fact that the news of Alex's passing had made it into nighttime host Jay Leno's joke monologue signified how deep and far-reaching Alex's death was and how it had emotionally touched so many people.

Why? Why were so many people so traumatized and saddened by the death of a parrot... a little bird that was no larger than a pigeon? His scientific accomplishments were astounding and he had been a trailblazer, proving beyond a doubt that animals are intelligent. But he represented something even more profound... something even more important. Alex was the "quintessential talking animal." He tapped into the primordial memory of our collective unconscious that remembers a time when animals physically talked to man... a time when man and animal lived together and shared mutual respect for one another. Some people may call that time the Garden of Eden when the animals talked to Adam and Eve, and others may call it the magical Land of Pan (Pangea). Whatever it is called, it did happen and it was real. Alex represented the possibility that we could get back in our hearts to that place of mutual love and respect, before evil and destruction separated us: Humankind from Nature. He was the archetypal talking animal that exuded unconditional love, and he captured our hearts and provided a loving place and a memory to which we could return within our own primordial souls.

Meeting Alex

I remember when I first met Alex in the late 1990s, and I especially remember the anticipation that I went through before actually meeting him. Wow, oh wow! I was going to meet a hero ... a legend. Irene and Alex were like rock stars in the bird world, and I was going to be among the lucky few to actually meet Alex and to be in his presence. Merlin and I had been invited to spend the weekend in Tucson with

Irene and she was planning to bring Alex home with her to join us. I was excited and nervous at the same time about the trip because I was afraid that he may not like me, since he had a reputation for liking tall, blonde human men. He didn't usually pay much attention to women, except for Irene and a few female trainers.

I had loved hearing Irene's stories and descriptions of Alex. Once she had described him as acting like a grouchy, disgruntled, little old man, clothed in a crumpled gray rain-coat, refusing to cooperate when he had to repeat the same experiments over and over and over again. Guess I would have acted like that too! At other times, he was like a little drill sergeant ordering the student trainers to retrieve this and that, or to take him somewhere. Then there were the sweet times when he said, "You be good. See you tomorrow. I love you," when Irene left the lab at night. I remember hearing that sweet little voice of his through the telephone when he hung out with Irene while we had our lengthy, weekly telephone conversations.

Merlin and I checked in at LaGuardia airport for our flight from New York City to Tucson, excited and ready for the trip! Of course, hanging out in airports that have lots of peo-ple and high ceilings was one of Merlin's favorite activities because she loved to make a shrill wolf call that reverberated against the walls and ceilings. And of course, there was always that one human goof-ball that would whistle back from the other end of the airport. Then once we were checked in and sitting at our gate, Merlin loved to show off her animal sound skills, which seemed to attract every child and adult-child in the airport. Merlin was like the Pied piper drawing crowds of people to her side and she loved every moment of it!

Once we arrived in Tucson, Irene took us to her house so that I could unpack and get Merle acclimated to Irene's home before meeting Alex. I pulled out Miss Merlin's portable perch and placed it near the window so that she could look out at the southwest scenery while preening herself for the big introduction. Then, I unpacked a few things and settled on the sofa to read a magazine. Finally, Irene arrived with a bird carrier in tow. She placed the carrier on top of a large black bird cage that was in her dining room, opened the carrier door and said, "Okay, Alex. Come on out."

There he was: Alex, standing on top of his weekend cage... larger than life. I slowly walked over to the cage. "Hello, Alex," I said. "I'm Maggie and this is Merlin. We are so excited to meet you!" He took one look at me and started to moan and groan. Then he twisted and shook his head up and down, and finally he threw up his lunch, all over the cage. To people who do not know birds, this means LOVE! Alex had taken to me! This was an honor because, as I had just stated, there were very few human women that attracted him.

But Merlin was not so honored, as she had never seen another parrot react to HER human in that way! She sat on her perch with both feet clamped onto the bar; her feathers were flat, almost skin-tight to the body; her eyes were large like saucers and she seemed in a trance while watching Alex throw up his lunch over HER human!

I did not know exactly what to do. I was very touched by Alex's reaction on one side, and then I could also feel the hurt and anger coming from Merlin. I felt as if I were walking a tightrope. Every time I went near Alex and picked him up, he got into his sexual, hormonal head-bobbing and lunch-throwing mode. So I would spend a few minutes with him and then for another few minutes, I hung out with Merlin across the room to practice her animal sounds.

Irene was used to Alex's sexual reactions to the male students in the lab, and so this reaction to me did not surprise her. However, I was not used to it because neither Merlin nor Sweetpea had reacted to me in this way since I was more like the mommy-caretaker for both of them. Often, the person who is the original nurturing caretaker for a parrot as a young chick turns out to be perceived in that way by the parrot, and then, another member of the household may become the object-of-desire or mate when the bird matures sexually. This is another example of how even though our parrots are domestically raised, it is extremely important to understand their wild instincts.

As the weekend progressed, Merle and Alex became much closer and they enjoyed talking 'at' each other. It went like this:

"What does the roooster say?" chimed Miss Merlin. She was relaxed on her perch with her feathers loosely hanging off of her body, but as she spoke, she stood tall and stretched out her neck to elongate her emphasis on "rooooster."

Alex looked over at Merlin from his large throne-cage and

answered, "Want paaah!"(pasta)

Merle twisted her neck and looked over at Alex with one eye, "Er! Er!... Er! Er!"

"Want corn," he said in response.

"What does the duck say?" asked Merlin.

"Want wheeeet!" responded Alex.

"Quack! Quack! Quack!" exclaimed Merlin.

"Want chair!" responded Alex.

"What does the cat say?" asked Merlin.

"Want showaaa," answered Alex.

Uh, huh, they were communicating. At least they were having fun and enjoying each other's company. This allowed Irene and me to go off shopping and exploring Tucson, as the parrots were left in their respective cages to further carry on with their very important conversation to change the world, or something. I will always remember that very special weekend with fondness.

COGNITIVE TRANSFERENCE

Alex could perform many of the same cognitive tasks as chimpanzees, dolphins, and five-year-old human children; but what astounded me the most about him was his ability to come up with understandings on his own. One of my favorite Alex stories was one where he proved to the Pepperberg Lab that he understood how to add, all on his own and without ever being taught.

Alex was competitive with his junior colleagues, and sometimes, he tried to mess them up in their training practice sessions. He would give them either the wrong answer... or answer their questions correctly before they could answer... or give them direction, such as telling them to "talk clearly," and so on. During an auditory number training session given to Griffin, big brother Alex decided to help out. In a normal session, the Grey student is told by the human trainer to "listen," and computer-generated clicks at certain numbers of intervals, such as four or five or one and so on, are sounded. Then the trainer asks, "How many [clicks]" did he hear? On this particular day the trainer was working with Griffin on the number TWO. The session went as follows:

Trainer: "Griffin, listen." Computer clicks twice: "click, click." "How many?"

Griffin refused to answer the question.

Trainer: "Griffin, listen." Computer clicks twice, "click, click." "How many?"

Griffin still refused to answer. Instead, Alex answered, "Four!"

"Alex, be quiet, please." said the trainer (thinking that Alex was just messing around and just threw out a number). "This is Griffin's session."

Trainer: "Griffin, listen." Computer clicks twice: "click, click." "How many?"

Again, Griffin refused to answer. "Six!" answered Alex.

Alex had proven that he, indeed, could add! He had added up the three computer-generated clicks of two to be six! And he did it all by himself! [1]

Alex was among many incredible animals that proved animal intelligence. Washoe, a famous chimpanzee that worked with Allen and Beatrice Gardner and then Dr. Roger Fouts, was the first non-human to communicate through the English language.[2] Previous studies had indicated that chimpanzees were not able to replicate the vocal sounds needed to physically "speak,"[3] but the Gardners took advantage of Washoe's natural body language skills and taught her to communicate through using American Sign Language (ASL). In total, she learned approximately 250 ASL signs. Not only did she learn the signs, but she could also put them together in meaningful ways. An example: she referred to the toilet as "dirty good," although her trainers had called it "potty chair;" and she referred to the refrigerator as "open food drink," while her trainers had called it "cold box."[4] Washoe died at 42 years old in 2007, just 6 weeks following Alex's death at 31 years old.

Over the past 30+ years, scientists have proven that animals are more than mere mindless automatons, incapable of any thought and feeling. We animal lovers who live on a day-to-day basis with our dogs, cats, rabbits, birds, horses, and so on, have always known this fact, but our stories have been disqualified as being anecdotal, and therefore, not important evidence. But it turns out that we are in good company. Charles Darwin believed that animals and other critters of nature were intelligent; they utilized cognitive and problem solving skills to survive, similar to humans. According to science writer Virginia Morell in her *National Geographic Magazine* article, "Minds of Their Own," Mr. Darwin went so far as to call earthworms "cognitive beings" because they had to make decisions on uses of different types of leafy matter.[5] Further, according to the article, his observations, as well as those of later researchers, were discarded in the early 20th century and labeled as "anecdotal." The research method for studying animals as machines then took over. But finally, the light has been switched back on and animals and other critters of nature are now being recognized as the intelligent and sentient beings that they always have been. Bravo!

WITNESSING TRUE LOVE

Shortly after I moved to Phoenix, Arizona in 2006, a pigeon couple, whom I named Lucy and Beau, started hanging out in my backyard. They always came together, except when one of them was on nest. They perched on the cement wall, preening, cooing, allo-preening, and kissing. They walked around the yard, shoulder to shoulder, bobbing their heads in unison, and when they stopped, they were always touching, whether by wings or beaks. When they took over my bird bath, they sat side by side, swishing the water onto their heads and then onto their backs. After bathing, they just sat there in the water, sometimes for as long as a half hour, as one and at peace... together.

Every time I saw them in the yard, I stopped what I was doing to watch them because there was something special about them. The love between these two birds was so strong that it often made me cry. If ever I were lucky enough to find a connection with a mate like that, even for 5 minutes, I would consider myself one of the luckiest humans.

Finally, they brought along their love-child chick, whom I named Junior. Lucy and Beau were such loving parents; they guided and taught Junior to do everything. All three pigeons were beautiful, but Junior had a fresh, young look, although he remained a little stiff and clumsy about many things. For example, he never really 'got it' about the bird bath. He knew it was a place to drink and bathe, but he never learned how to plop and relax in it.

One morning I noticed that Lucy could not fly off of the ground, and after a closer look, I saw that she had been hit by a car and was not able to walk. I promptly threw towels in a cardboard box and swooped her up to go to the wildlife rehabilitation expert down the street. Jeanne, the rehabber, gave Lucy food, water, and medication. She informed me that since there was feeling in Lucy's feet, there was a possibility that she could heal. I prayed for Lucy and placed her name on every Internet prayer board that I could find, and

I called Jeanne every other day to see how Lucy was doing.

Meanwhile, Beau returned to my backyard every morning with Junior in tow. They perched a few inches apart on the cement wall, and Junior followed daddy Beau around the yard to peck at this and look at that. Then, he followed Dad to the bird bath. He was finally getting the rhythm of bathing, with a swish of water on his head and then a swish of water on his back, but he was still awkward and not sure about squatting in the water and relaxing.

As the days passed, Jeanne, the rehabilitator, informed me that Lucy was becoming more and more despondent: she was not eating and seemed extremely depressed. At the same time, Beau seemed so lonely in my backyard. Although much of his time was spent guiding Junior, he came to the yard more often than before, and he sat alone for long periods of time at the same place on the cement wall where he had once courted Lucy. Finally, I received word that Jeanne had euthanized Lucy since the bird had been suffering so badly from pain and depression.

After speaking with Jeanne, I put the telephone back on the receiver, lay on my white sofa, and sobbed all afternoon for the loss of that beautiful pigeon. I sobbed for Beau and Junior who had lost their mate and parent. I sobbed for myself because I missed the beautiful sight of a pigeon couple in love, reminding me every day that true love does exist, and it is possible.

As the months passed, I noticed only one pigeon coming to

my yard: Junior. He perched on the roof to watch me as I cleaned the bird bath and put out a little seed. I talked to him as he flitted from one side of the yard to the other to follow me. Then it finally dawned on me that he was now alone. Beau had gone to the other side to be with his true love, and their love-chick was the only one left.

A few weeks later, as I was leaving my yard, I noticed Junior floating like a duck in a nearby swimming pool, soaking wet and terrified. It was a miracle that I happened to see him when I did and that he had not drowned. It felt as if I were meant to be there at that split moment to save him. I fished him out with a net, wrapped him up, and rushed him to Jeanne's house. She gave him antibiotics and placed him in an incubator to dry out, and I returned him to my yard the next day. I opened the carrier box and he flew into the wall: he could not fly. So I recaptured and returned him to Jeanne who determined that his wing was only bruised. So I agreed to leave him with Jeanne to heal, to bond with a new group of pigeons, and to start a new life.

Beau and Lucy are back together in heaven and their love-chick was given a fresh new start. This whole incredible experience helped me to see that God does indeed have an individual plan for everyone, including a little pigeon.

J used to feed pigeons in New York City and I loved them there, but my one-on-one experience of getting to know Lucy, Beau, and Junior opened my eyes as to how calm, loving, and gentle these birds really are. Actually, pigeons are part of the dove family (Columbidae family) and they are called Rock Doves. Their ancestors lived among coastal cliffs and rock ledges in West Asia, Europe, and North Africa, where they nested in little cubby holes to raise their young. As a result, today's feral pigeons instinctively flourish in the nooks, crannies, and cubby holes of tall buildings of large cities across the world. But this may be considered a curse by many city-living people who vilify them as pests and nuisances. Woody Allen's 1980 movie, "Stardust Memories," summed it up perfectly when he referred to New York pigeons as "rats with wings[6]." And their poor public image carried forward from there. Pigeon control pundits have tried to scare people to believe that pigeons are disease-ridden, although authorities from the Department of Health and CDC have claimed that they pose little public health risk[7]. Nevertheless, the poor city pigeon has been thrust into a tug-of-war between the pigeon haters and lovers.

And now, many city governments have stepped into the battle against pigeons. For example, it is against the law to feed pigeons in London and anyone caught in the act, especially in Trafalgar Square, will face possible prosecution and a steep fine[8]. City officials have used a combination of tactics to decrease the bird population in the Square, such as removing any available food from the ground and utilizing Harris hawks and megaphones to scare off the birds. They estimate that there has been a substantial bird population drop since the inception of the program in 2003. However, many pigeon advocates have claimed that the birds died off by long, agonizing starvation deaths, instead of flying away.[9] The usual strategy of assuming that a bird will go elsewhere to find food when the availability is cut off does not always work with pigeons. That is because of their homing instincts and tendency not to leave their home grounds.

Anti-pigeon feeding laws have also been entertained by New York City officials, and some private citizens have apparently taken pigeon removal into their own hands. In addition to poisons and gels that have been planted by some land-lords to drive off the pigeons, there are reports that thousands of these birds have been illegally netted and removed from the streets. Some believe that many of them are sold as live targets for the pigeon shoots that still exist in Pennsylvania.[10] As discussed in Chapter 10, the pigeons at these live-bird gun clubs have little chance of survival when they are shot by sport hunters practicing their gun skills. Then they are either kicked or stomped on by young children, if they did not die from the marksman gun shots.

In spite of some negative human attitudes about pigeons, these birds have done so many good things for humankind. Before the telegraph, they were used to carry messages. White doves are now released with the opening ceremonies of the Olympic Games because their pigeon ancestor cousins were used to transport messages about the Olympic Game results during the times of the Roman Empire. They were also used as messenger carriers during both World Wars, and as a result, they saved thousands and thousands of soldiers' lives.[11]

One of the most celebrated pigeons, Cher Ami, flew 12 missions in World War I that saved thousands of American and Frenchmen's lives.[12] As a result, he was awarded the French 'Croix de Guerre' for his valiant service. One of his most famous feats was on the day of October 13, 1918, when he delivered a message from Major Charles Whittlesey, commander of a battalion of American soldiers in the 77th Infantry Division. Major Whittlesey and his 200 men were trapped by enemy fire on a hillside in France. The American artillery was firing rounds and rounds of fire at the enemy to protect Whittlesey and his men, but they did not know where the American troops were located. The problem was that their bullets were actually raining on Major Whittlesey and his men, in addition to the enemy. Cher Ami was released into the air with a note about their whereabouts attached to his leg. In spite of heavy German gunfire attempts to shoot him down, Cher Ami managed to fly high above the range of the conflict to deliver the message. This bird-hero flew 25 miles in just 25 minutes to save 200 of the doomed infantrymen from both enemy and collateral fire.

Pigeons are smarter than they have been given credit. Pigeon researchers have found that they can recognize 26 letters of the alphabet. When given photograph tests, it was determined that they could differentiate between various photographs and even recognize individuals within a photograph.[13]

But pigeons, or Rock Doves, are most famously associated with Biblical references where they symbolize peace and the Holy Spirit. Most notably, Noah sent out a Rock Dove to determine if the waters from the Great Flood had lessened:

"Then he sent out a dove, to see if the waters had lessened on the earth. But the dove could find no place to alight and perch, and it returned to him in the ark, for there was water all over the earth. Putting out his hand, he caught the dove and drew it back to him inside the ark. He waited seven days more and again sent the dove out from the ark. In the evening the dove came back to him, and there in its bill was a plucked-off olive leaf. So Noah knew that the waters had lessened on earth." Genesis 8: 8-11 The New American Bible. Catholic Bible Press, a division of Thomas Nelson Publishers, Inc. Nashville, Tennessee.

God came down to earth in the form of a dove to bless Jesus at his baptism by John the Baptist:

"I did not know him, but the one who sent me to baptize with water told me, 'On whomever you see the Spirit come down and remain, he is the one who will baptize with the Holy Spirit.' Now I have seen and testified that he is the Son of God. John testified further, saying, 'I saw the Spirit come down like a dove from the sky and remain upon him.'" John 1: 32-34 The New American Bible. Catholic Bible Press, a division of Thomas Nelson Publishers, Inc. Nashville, Tennessee.

It confounds me that this gentle pigeon prey animal is so honored and revered from so many perspectives, but yet, it continues to be defiled and denigrated by other forces, and with the same level of vigor. In her *New York Times* article called "Noble Eagles, Nasty Pigeons, Biased Humans," Natalie Angier calls the act of disapproving of one type of animal over another "biobigotry."[14] She defines it as: "the persistent and often irrational desire to be surrounded only by those species of which one approves, and to exclude any animals, plants, and other life forms that one finds offensive." Nasty pigeons are called "rats with wings." Opportunistic Brown-headed cowbirds are called nature's parasites. Raucous European starlings and bullying crows are just plain nuisances. But in fact, they really are only acting on the instinct that Mother Nature gave them. Pigeons tend to crowd the cities because the tall city building nooks and crannies replicate the homes of their cliff-dwelling ancestors. Cowbirds' ancestors followed herds of buffalo in search of certain insects that the buffalo stirred up while grazing in the plains. Since the buffalo traveled long distances and the cow-birds had to follow them, these birds did not have the time to stop to build nests and raise babies. Instead, they learned to leave their eggs in others' nests to carry on their gene pool.[15] European starlings and crows are highly social flock animals. Instead of trying to understand them, we just keep cutting down their territories, but yet complaining when they encroach upon ours because they have few natural forest homes left. Sometimes it makes me wonder who real-ly is the kinder, gentler species.

PARALLEL LIVES IN MY YARD

There was a large cholla cactus tree in my Phoenix front yard that seemed to be a very popular piece of nesting real estate for many southwestern birds. I have no idea how a bird could get around a tree like that, but they did like masters. I loved to watch the little finches and wrens fly around that thing and plop down, so easily maneuvering their tiny little legs around those sticky, sharp thorns. The "owner" of my cholla cactus was a beautiful Curve-billed thrasher. I called him Sir Thrasher because of his great skill at protecting the tree. His mate, whom I named Lady Thrasher, had only one leg and absolutely no tail feathers, which she had probably lost from nesting and moving around so much in that cactus tree. Sir and Lady Thrasher were quite a pair. They woke me up every morning with their "weet, weet... weet, weet" contact calls. Like clockwork, I constantly heard their early-morning "weet, weet" song through the exhaust fan in my kitchen while making my breakfast and the morning MASH for Merle, Pea and Kyo. Their sound gave me a feeling of well-being, perhaps because it was consistent all day, every day, and it had melded with the overall atmosphere and energy of my home.

I truly admired Lady Thrasher. She whipped around that yard, grabbing a twig here and a leaf there, to build their home nest. I watched her perch on my cement wall, completely balanced, again with no tail and only one leg. Sometimes, when perching on a tree, she leaned against a branch to give herself extra support. As I watched, I wondered how much energy and vitality it must take for her to get through the day, but it did not seem to bother her at all. Her energy and attitude reminded me of my friend Sonia who was battling cancer. No matter what impediment tried to get in their way, my friend Sonia and Lady Thrasher-bird seemed to thrive.

Lady Thrasher stopped coming to the tree because a neighborhood cat started stalking the yard, but I knew she was still around because I could constantly hear the "weet, weet" calls, back and forth throughout the neighborhood between Sir and Lady Thrasher. She continued to return to the yard to drink and bathe in the bird bath, but she never returned to the tree; therefore, I assumed she must have made a new nest. All the while, Sir Thrasher continued to protect that tree, his territory, even though there was no nesting activity in it. I think he may have been sleeping at night in the nest because I remember a "weet, weet" sound, as well as some rustling, late one night when I watered the front yard. It sounded as if I had disturbed him.

The next spring Sir Thrasher attracted a new mate, whom I named Ms. Bird. Together, their "weet, weet" song medley once again filled my house after a long cold winter. They promptly laid eggs and a young thrasher chick was born. I watched Sir Thrasher and Ms. Bird feed that chick, day after day. I was so thrilled to be able to witness its progress! Every time I heard the noise level increase by decibels in the front yard, I knew that the parents had just delivered some yummy morsels. So I took breaks from my writing to witness the feedings. Sometimes Merlin and Sweetpea sat on my shoulders, as we watched from our window the 'goings on' in that cholla tree.

As the days passed and the baby got older, he started to climb around the tree to look out and explore. "Little chick, will you fledge today?" I wondered. The anticipation of the big day, the day when that little bird was going to take a leap of faith, was building. Finally, once there were no more sounds coming from the tree, I knew he had fledged. And I had missed it! Oh no!

Weeks following, Sir Thrasher and Ms. Bird flew around the yard and neighborhood, taking turns at teaching their chick his living skills. Sir Thrasher seemed to be the main teacher as Ms. Bird repeatedly returned to the nest, probably preparing to brood more eggs.

One morning a hawk came into the yard and snatched the baby away, right in front of all of us. I screamed and cried because that little chick had become a part of my extended family. Merlin, Sweetpea, and Kyo became very quiet because it happened right outside of their window. It was so close... so graphic... so upsetting.

Four days later, as I drove into my driveway, I noticed a dead bird lying on the sidewalk in front of my yard. It was Sir Thrasher who had been hit by a car. I grabbed some paper towels, wrapped him up, and hugged him because he had meant so much to me for a long time. Then I buried him in the yard. He had been family and I was devastated.

Two family deaths in the same week are difficult for anyone to handle, including a bird. Ms. Bird was beside herself. Day after day, week after week, all she did was sit in her nest, looking out blankly. There were no more "weet, weet" sounds. She took short breaks to find something to eat, and then promptly returned to the nest. When she was off eating, I snuck over to look in the nest. It was empty. She was sitting on an empty nest day after day, with no eggs... no mate... and no chick. She seemed listless and depressed.

My home felt different. There were no more "weet, weet" sounds to awaken me and to fill the kitchen while preparing morning breakfast. I felt so sad! I could feel Ms. Bird's pain and sorrow. Day after day, there she was, sitting in that empty nest. The normal yard activity was going on around her, but she didn't react to anything. I got the feeling from her that she just did not want to live any longer.

I walked outside every morning to speak to her and send her little loving hugs. "It will get better, Ms. Bird," I thought to her. I pretended in my head and heart that I was holding and comforting her. As I held her in my heart, I imagined that I was helping her release her sadness and pain.

Approximately one month later, I noticed a new thrasher hanging out at the nest. My Ms. Bird had gone out and found herself a new man! Wowee zowie! This was thrilling. She sat in the nest and he flew around the yard, investigating the cholla tree and another cactus where I frequently left food. They seemed happy for a day. Then that evening, she chased him away. She did not like him! Oh, well.

As the weeks progressed, she stayed away from the nest more and more, but I could finally hear the "weet, weet" sounds in the neighborhood. She had energy and was out there searching. Her travails of looking for a mate reminded me of myself when I spent those tireless evenings in the 1980s going out every night, wondering if I would ever find someone to love. In New York City, you had to be out there, in the sea of people, in the bars and restaurants, if you wanted a shot at meeting someone. Ms. Bird's challenge was not all that different. She had to be out there in the neighborhood and across neighborhoods, in search of a single thrasher male who may have lost a mate or who had not yet settled on one.

During the weeks that Ms. Bird was absent looking for a mate, I remarked to Merlin, Pea, and Kyo that I missed the "weet, weet" sound. That evening, Merlin started saying "weet, weet." I could not believe it! She understood what I had said! How smart is that? "Weet, weet" has now become our in-house contact call.

Finally, Ms. Bird found a suitable mate and they made their home in the cholla tree in my front yard. They had a beautiful baby chick, and I now hear "weet, weet" sounds bustling all over and around my house, inside and out. Once again, all is in balance.

Sometimes it is emotionally draining being as sensitive as I am. Some of my friends just do not seem to understand. They tell me, "Maggie, that's nature!" when I lament over a lost backyard critter. That's right. It is nature, and it's also nature when a human child or parent gets hurt or dies. Should we respond, "That's nature," when we hear about a human tragedy? No. We extend compassion and feeling for the family. We see them as individuals. But when we lump all of Nature up into one word, one group, we don't have to feel anything. We can say, "Oh Maggie, that's nature." That thrasher was in deep depression and pain over the loss of her mate and baby. The grackle in Upstate New York was devastated at the loss of his mate.

We humans tend to intellectualize, believing that we are the only thinking/feeling species that matters. We are not. There is pain and suffering going on everywhere on this earth, but when we allow our hearts to open to have compassion for everything around us, to extend love to every creature, the world becomes a happier place.

I am not trying to bring animals and other critters of nature to the level of human beings. God gave humankind responsibility for stewardship of the animals, to care for all of His creation with love, honor, and respect. Instead of spinning our wheels intellectually fighting over extremist ideas of making animals into little people or changing their legal status, let's open our hearts and feel compassion for them. We need to see them as the thinking/feeling creatures that they are. We need to really see them as the individuals that they are. We need to take responsibility for our part of our covenant with God to ensure the welfare of our animals and other critters of the Earth.

"The just man takes care of his beast, but the heart of the wicked is merciless." Proverbs 12:10

"Are not five sparrows sold for two pennies? Yet not one of them is forgotten in God's sight." Luke 12:6

Incredible Goodness and Unconditional Love of Animals

In the Biblical story of Cain and Abel, Adam and Eve produced two sons: Cain and Abel. Cain became a farmer and he grew vegetables and grains. Abel loved animals and he became the shepherd who watched over the family flock. When it was time to make a sacrifice to the Lord, Abel presented his most prized and loved "firstling" from his flock. Cain presented some grains from his field. God accepted Abel's sacrifice, but He rejected the offering from Cain. Many people have interpreted this story to mean that Cain's sacrifice was rejected because it was not the blood sacrifice of an animal, which was often made in the Old Testament as atonement for the forgiveness of a sin.[16] However, when one could not afford an animal to sacrifice, there were provisions that allowed a human to substitute grain for the life of an animal (Leviticus 5:11-13). Therefore, it is not the fact that Cain did not sacrifice an animal, but instead, I believe it is because he did not give a sacrifice from his heart. He did not offer his most loved and prized possession, as his brother had, to show his appreciation to God.

Animal sacrifice was very common throughout the Old Testament because the Lord loved humankind so much that he allowed humans to substitute animals' lives for their own, to atone for their human sins.[17] Adam and Eve were the first to offer a prized lamb to demonstrate their appreciation to God for all that He had given. Throughout the Old Testament there was a specific procedure that had to be followed where the one who sacrificed had to take responsibility for it by: finding a pure animal, being connected with it, and then killing it himself. The sacrifice had to mean something and come from the human's heart in faith, in order for it to work.

In the New Testament, the Lord again demonstrated His deep love for humankind by giving up His son, Jesus Christ, to serve as the final sacrifice for the forgiveness of sins. Jesus served as the Lord's symbolic human-animal offering, as he was called the "Lamb of God." Jesus provided the ultimate sacrifice of his life so that humans of faith no longer had to do their own sacrificing. Instead, they were saved by the sacrament of his body and blood.

When there is a sacred sacrifice, the one doing it must operate from his heart. Accordingly, the one being sacrificed must also be clean, pure, and good in the heart. Jesus was willing from his heart to come down to Earth to be sacrificed by his Father for all of humankind. The animals, although at lower spiritual levels than Jesus but yet pure in heart, were willing to give up their lives as substitutes on behalf of humans, until the ultimate offering of the "Lamb of God." Since Jesus provided the final and ultimate sacrifice, the animals no longer needed to be sacrificed for humans' sins; therefore, Jesus also died for the animals, as well as for us humans.

I am not trying to place animals on the physical or spiritual level of Jesus, but I am pointing out their goodness and their ultimate willingness to give of themselves for the Greater Good. The animals could only atone for one sin at time, but the Son of God's sacrifice was for all sins of those who believe in him. I believe that by giving up his only Son, the Lord also demonstrated His love for ALL of His creation, which includes the animals.

We animal people constantly witness our companions' ultimate goodness through their unconditional love. I am reminded of it often when I hear Merlin say to me, "I love you SO hard! It's all that matters."

Spend time with nature in your backyard.

chapter twelve

BRINGING BACK THE MAGIC

Shortly after I moved to Phoenix in early 2006, I purchased a beautiful albino French Lop bunny rabbit. I named him Anassas, and Nassie became his nickname. At the time, I was living in a wall-to-wall carpeted house, and so I had to cover the floor with plastic wrap so that Nassie would not mess up his room. Then I purchased a large three-story pen so that he would have lots of space in which to run around.

Nassie was my first French Lop. He had such a comical face with those floppy ears that floated around in the air when he jumped, twisted, and turned. I enjoyed watching him eat because I could see his large pink tongue that stood out from all of that pure white fur. Sometimes I thought I could see him smile! I had forgotten how gorgeous albino rabbits were with their pink eyes.

Nassie had two favorite toys. His stuffed, white bunny rabbit served as his best buddy; he preened it at night and slept with it. He also had a three-dimensional, stuffed, cotton pyramid toy that seemed to answer some sexual needs, and he took that little pyramid everywhere with him. He had a nightly ritual where he held the pyramid toy in his teeth and ran up the platform to the very top of the cage; he sat upright on his hind legs and then lifted his head three times while stretching his neck and holding the toy in his teeth. Then, he ran to the bottom of the cage; sat upright again on his hind legs; and then lifted his head into the air three times.

When I first got Nassie, I frequently brought him out into the living room to play with me on the sofa. We played hide and seek and peek-a-boo, some of my Grey guys' favorite games too. I absolutely loved that little bunny!

A few months after getting him, I came down with a severe case of bronchitis, and I could not seem to get rid of it. My doctor and I worked through many scenarios, but finally after some tests, we discovered that I was highly allergic to rabbits. Oh no! Rabbits had meant so much to me! How could I be allergic to a little creature whom I absolutely adored? Then I remembered that I had been sick a lot as a young child and slept often under vaporizer tents, in order to cure the congestion in my lungs. Now, I realize those bad colds may have really been allergic reactions to Mr. Tewillager and all of the other rabbits whom I adored, but no one had ever figured it out.

Determined not to give Nassie up, I decided to confine him to his room, and then to protect my lungs, I wore a face mask while cleaning and playing with him. Nassie was lonely without a rabbit pal, but I knew that I could possibly get

extremely sick if two rabbits lived with me in the house. Nassie's girlfriend Josie was living with Sonia and we had planned to bring her in to live with him, as soon as I got settled with having one rabbit. But once I learned how allergic I was to rabbits, it became obvious that bringing her in would be a bad idea, and so Josie continued to live with Sonia in Scottsdale, Arizona. Finally, after two years of this situation, we decided that Nassie and Josie would be happier together in a loving rabbit sanctuary in Sedona.

 Letting go of Nassie was an emotionally-drenching experience, but I knew it was the right decision. He and Josie were ecstatically happy together in the hills of Sedona. They were free to socialize with lots of other bunnies, as well as to run, jump, and hop all over the grounds. Six months later, Nassie died of a liver infection.

I had come full circle, having another white rabbit in my life. My mother's death had been so devastating that I blocked out many of my childhood memories, but Nassie's presence brought back the memories of the happy, magical times. Nassie inspired me to stop procrastinating and to write this book!

In life, God gives us experiences, both good and bad, which help us to twist and turn and bring ourselves to a higher level of behavioral and spiritual understanding. Most of us have had difficult experiences with our families and within

Merlin's first dinner party at home.

Merlin's first Round Table Group party.

childhood. No matter how dysfunctional our lives are, what really matters is what we do with what we have inherited... how we react to and resolve what was thrown our way. We are responsible for what we create in our lives.

During my days in corporate packaged-goods marketing in the 1980s, many focus group moderators and other researchers liked to work with me because I believed in looking at my brands and new products through the eyes of the consumer. I believed in the concept: "perception is reality." In short, no matter what the brand was like, what mattered more was how the consumer saw it. This also is true on an individual life basis, as our thoughts and feelings create our realities. Positive thought and love can help us build a more compassionate world.

In these times when everything appears to be falling apart around us, the more we connect with Nature, the more grounded and calm we will be. I now ask you to help me spread the word about a new way of looking at Nature and all of its critters, including our animal companions. If each one of us becomes connected with just our backyards, and then, our number grows to millions of people, we can revolutionize the way in which the world sees animals and Nature.

Spend time in your backyard under a shady tree and observe Mother Nature at her best. Open your senses and see the vibrant colors: the combination of the grass, flowers, plants and trees. Watch the insects as they slowly meander through the pine straw or flit from one flower to the next. Watch the busy squirrels and chipmunks scurrying about the yard. Open your ears to the medley of birdsong and learn to associate specific sounds by bird species. Smell the aroma of the flowers and recently cut grass. Touch the bark of the tree and feel its texture. Observe the critters in your backyard. Study up on their behavior and try to understand what their lives may be like. Open your heart and see them as intelligent and sentient beings that have purposeful lives of their own.

Our companion animals are our teachers, helping us to see that there is more in life than our mundane daily activities. There is a physical and spiritual world waiting to be discovered, once we pull back the veil. Magic is everywhere in our lives, and all we need to do is open our eyes to see it. Let's do it together!

*"If you have men who will exclude any
of God's creatures from the shelter
of compassion and pity, you will
have men who will deal likewise
with their fellow men."*

St. Francis of Assisi

FOOTNOTES AND REFERENCES

CHAPTER ONE
Incidences and conversations were based on my father's notes about what happened, plus my personal memories.

CHAPTER TWO
1. Phrases from the pop song, "Smile," which came from the 1936 Charlie Chaplain movie, *Modern Times.* Chaplain composed the music and John Turner and Geoffrey Parsons wrote the words. Source: Wikipedia: http://en.wikipedia.org/wiki/Smile_(song)

CHAPTER FOUR
1. Collinge, William Ph.D. 1997. "Chapter 9: Massage Therapy & Bodywork: Healing Through Touch." The American Holistic Health Association *Complete Guide to Alternative Medicine.* Chapter 9, page 16. American Holistic Health Association. Anaheim, California.
http://www.healthy.net/collinge/massage.htm

CHAPTER FIVE
1. Information on Wilmington: http://www.wilmington.net/;
http://insiders.com/wilmington/main-attractions2.htm
2. Wentworth by the Sea history: http://www.wentworth.com/about/ wentworth-history.aspx
3. Lumina Pavilion history: http://www.blockade-runner.com/ lumina_daze.shtml;
http://www.wrightsville.com/luminia_days_at_wrightsville_beach.htm;
http://insiders.com/wilmington/sb-getting.htm

CHAPTER SIX
1. Excerpts from President Carter's "malaise speech." July 15, 1979.
http://millercenter.org/scripps/archive/speeches/detail/3402

CHAPTER SEVEN
1. Tintagel Castle and Merlin's cave: http://www.britainexpress.com/
counties/cornwall/castles/tintagel.htm
2. Information on African Grey parrots: http://www.AfricanGreys.com;
Wright, Maggie (Margaret T.). *African Grey Parrots: A Complete Pet Owner's Manual.* Barron's Educational Series, Inc. Hauppauge, New York, 2001.
3. Houlihan, Jane (VP Research); Thayer PhD, Kris (Sr. scientist); Klein, Jennifer (Chemist, Environmental Working Group). May, 2003. "Canaries in the Kitchen: Teflon Toxicosis," "EWG finds heated Teflon pans can turn toxic faster than DuPont claims." Environmental Working Group Research. Washington, D.C. http://www.ewg.org/reports/toxicteflon ; http://tuberose.com/Teflon.html
Douglass, William Campbell II MD. "Are scented candles dangerous?" The Douglass Report. 1994-2008. Baltimore, Maryland. http://www.douglassre-port.com/deardd/080903.html

CHAPTER EIGHT
1. N'Kisi Project: Aimee Morgana and her African Grey N'Kisi, collaborate with Dr. Rupert Sheldrake: http://www.sheldrake.org/papers/Animals/parrot_abs.html
2. Bekoff, Marc. *Minding Animals: Awareness, Emotions and Heart.* Oxford University Press, New York, New York, 2002. Page 55.

CHAPTER NINE
1. Babatundi Olatunji was a great Nigerian musician and spiritual leader who taught many people about drumming and African culture.
http://en.wikipedia.org/wiki/Babatunde_Olatunji;
http://www.olatunjimusic.com/;
http://www.numoonus.com/Baba/Olatunji.html
2. Bash-Bish Falls, Mt. Washington State Park, Massachusetts:
http://www.berkshireweb.com/sports/parks/bash.html
3. Memories of 911. Personal conversations with Gail Langsner, along with newspaper account: Carol Cole. 2002. "Amazing pet rescue brings a little peace and happiness." News-Star.com. last updated 2:13 a.m. Wednesday, September 11, 2002.
4. Maggie Wright. "Camelot Conference Summary." *Grey Play Round Table African Grey Magazine.* Winter 2002 Issue. Equatorial Group, Ltd. Phoenix, AZ.

CHAPTER TEN

1. Victor J. Tremblay, Carol Horton Tremblay. 2005. *The U.S. Brewing Industry: Data and Economic Analysis.* MIT Press, Chapter 6, pp 140-144.
2. "At long last, Pa bill would outlaw live pigeon shoots." 2006. Network.bestfriends.org.
http://network.bestfriends.org/legalanimal/news/8821.html
3. Pfaltz, Dr. Kay. 2008. "The Guardian Campaign." http://www.guardian-campaign.com/k_pfaltz.html;
http://www.guardiancampaign.com/index.html
4. Genny Wall. 2008. "Using the legal term 'Guardian,' rather than 'Owner,' Is this necessary, or even a good idea?" *AFA Watchbird*, Volume XXIX, Number 4, 2002. http://proaviculture.com/guardian.htm
5. Grandin, Temple. 2002. "Animals Are Not Things: A View on Animal Welfare Based on Neurological Complexity." Paper presented at a discussion on whether or not animals should be property. Colorado State University, Colorado Springs, CO.
http://www.grandin.com/welfare/animals.are.not.things.html
6. Richard L. Cupp, Jr. 2007. "A Dubious Grail: Seeking Tort Law Expansion and Limited Personhood as Stepping Stones Toward Abolishing Animals' Property Status." *SMU Law Review* Winter 2007. Southern Methodist University. (60 *SMU Law Review* 3 [2007]). Dallas, Texas. Page 1.
http://nabrlawlive.madwolf.com/Resources/LawReviewArticles/tabid/622/Default.aspx
7. Richard L. Cupp, Jr. 2007. "A Dubious Grail: Seeking Tort Law Expansion and Limited Personhood as Stepping Stones Toward Abolishing Animals' Property Status." *SMU Law Review* Winter 2007. Southern Methodist University. (60 *SMU Law Review* 3 [2007]). Dallas, Texas. Page 1.
8. http://www.nabr.org/AnimalLaw/Guardianship/index.htm
9. "West Virginia Committee Adopts Anti-Pet Legislation: Nearly All Pets Restricted Under Bill." 2005. Pet Industry Joint Advisory Council (PIJAC). March 30, 2005, (WV SB 277). http://pijac.org/files/public/WVS277.05.E.pdf
10. Maggie Wright. 2005. "The Power of One Voice," Issue 012. *Nature's Corner Magazine*, Equatorial Group, Ltd. Phoenix, AZ. Page 28.
11. Richard l. Cupp, Jr., 2007. "A Dubious Grail: Seeking Tort Law Expansion and Limited Personhood as Stepping Stones Toward Abolishing Animals' Property Status," Winter 2007. *SMU Law Review.* Southern Methodist University Dedman School of Law, page 5.
http://nabrlawlive.madwolf.com/Resources/LawReviewArticles/tabid/622/Default.aspx
12. http://www.nabrlaw.org/Personhood/OwnershipvGuardianship/tabid/634/Default.aspx
13. Jeffrey Stinson, 2008. "Activists pursue basic legal rights for great apes," *USA Today.* July 15, 2008. Page 7A.

14. Jeffrey Stinson, 2008. "Activists pursue basic legal rights for great apes," *USA Today*. July 15, 2008. Page 7A.
15. Laura Lorek, 2001. "Robots: Our helpers or replacements?" ZDNet Australia. September 09, 2001.
http://www.zdnet.com.au/news/business/print.htm?TYPE=story&AT=12 0219028-139023166t-110000004c
16. Laura Lorek, 2001. "Robots: Our helpers or replacements?" ZDNet Australia. September 09, 2001.
http://www.zdnet.com.au/news/business/print.htm?TYPE=story&AT=12 0219028-139023166t-110000004c
17. Temple Grandin: www.Grandin.com
18. http://animalsclubfreedom.org/index.html;
http://www.stopanimalid.org/
19. http://animalid.aphis.usda.gov/nais/index.shtml
20. http://www.nonais.org/
21. http://www.nonais.org; "Local Farmer States Opposition to NAIS." 2007. www.wickedlocal.comhttp://www.wickedlocal.com/harvard/archive/x2119540676; http://libertyark.net/

Recommended Materials to study (Educate yourself to protect your pets):
http://proaviculture.com/guardian.htm
http://www.grandin.com/welfare/animals.are.not.things.html
http://www.pet-law.com/
http://www.ncraoa.com/AR_AW_WhatYouShouldKnow.html
http://www.freewebs.com/animalrightsandyou/
http://www.animalscam.com/
http://saveourdogs.net/animalrights.html
http://www.animalwelfarecouncil.com/html/aw/rights.php
http://www.furcommission.com/resource/perspect999bd.htm
http://capwiz.com/naiatrust/home/
http://www.naiaonline.org/
http://www1.umn.edu/humanrts/peace/senate.html
http://www.ncraoa.com/articles/AR/GuardianshipTenPointList.pdf
http://www.mofed.org/Bob-Vella.html
http://www.ncraoa.com/Guardians.html
http://www.stopanimalid.org/links/organizationsopposed.php
http://www.agweekly.com/articles/2006/04/14/news/ag_news/news02.txt
http://libertyark.net/articles/givens-081707.html
http://animalsclubfreedom.org
http://www.NoNais.org

LISTING OF U.S. LOCALITIES THAT HAVE ADOPTED
ORDINANCES TO CHANGE "OWNERSHIP" LANGUAGE TO
"GUARDIANSHIP:"
• Santa Clara, CA (April, 2006)
• Bloomington, IN (January, 2006)
• St. Louis, MO (August 9, 2004)
• Albany, CA (June 7, 2004)
• Wanaque, NJ (May 13, 2004)
• Marin County, CA (December 2003)
• Sebastopol, CA (December, 2003)
• San Francisco, CA (January 13, 2003)
• Amherst, MA (April 24, 2002)
• Menomonee Falls, WI (March 11, 2002)
• Sherwood, AR (September 24, 2001)
• State of Rhode Island (July 5, 2001 in constitution)
• West Hollywood, CA (February 19, 2001)
• Berkeley, CA (February 27, 2001)
• Boulder, CO (July 12, 2000)
"While this campaign is marketed as a feel-good exercise, this 'simple' change
in language elevates animals above their current status as property—with
potentially enormous legal implications." NABR Animal Law Section
SOURCE: http://www.nabrlaw.org/Personhood/
OwnershipvGuardianship/tabid/634/Default.aspx

CHAPTER ELEVEN
1. Leigh Ann Hartsfield, 2008. "My Brilliant Friend," Issue 014, *Nature's
Corner Magazine*, Equatorial Group, Ltd, Phoenix, AZ. Pp 9-11.
2. Peter Colen, 2008."Washoe: The Mother of Invention," Issue 014, *Nature's
Corner Magazine*, Equatorial Group, Ltd. pp 38-39.
3. "Washoe Chimpanzee." Wikipedia. (referring to the Gua and Vicki chimpanzee experiments). http://en.wikipedia.org/wiki/Washoe_(chimpanzee)
4. "Washoe Chimpanzee." Wikipedia. http://en.wikipedia.org/wiki/
Washoe_(chimpanzee)
5. Virginia Morell, 2008. "Minds of Their Own," March 2008 issue, *National
Geographic Magazine*. Washington, D.C. pp.37-61.
6. "Stardust Memories." Movie written/directed by Woody Allen. 1980.
New York, New York.
7. Michael McNeil, Center for Disease Control (CDC). http://www.urban-
wildlifesociety.org/zoonoses/ExprtsRePijZoonos.html;
http://cathrynsworld.com/projects.php;
Dr. Anthony A. Pilny, DVM, Dipl ABVP. 2007. "Understanding Zoonotic
Diseases of Pigeons in NYC." http://peopleforpigeons.blogspot.com/2007/
11/understanding-zoonotic-diseases-of.html
8. "Feeding Trafalgar's Pigeons Illegal," 2003. BBC News, United Kingdom.

November 7, 2003. http://news.bbc.co.uk/2/hi/uk_news/england/london/3275233.stm

9. "Tests Show Pigeons are Starving," 2007. BBC News, United Kingdom. December 11, 2007. http://news.bbc.co.uk/2/hi/uk_news/england/london/7138070.stm

10. Angela Montefinise and Cathy Burke, 2008. "Fresh Pigeon Snit." *New York Post.* January 6, 2008.
http://www.nypost.com/seven/01062008/news/regionalnews/fresh_pigeon_snit_828426.htm;
"Unlawful Pigeon Nettings Continue as New York City Does Nothing," 2007.
New York Bird Club, June 27, 2007.
http://newyorkbirdclub.blogspot.com/2007/06/pigeon-nettings-in-new-york.html

11. "Homing Pigeons' Wartime Accomplishments Celebrated on Anniversary of WWI Battle," 2008. Chicago Tribune. May 31, 2008.
http://www.chicagotribune.com/news/local/chi-homing-pigeon-sjun01,0,7195430.story?track=rss

12. "Cher Ami," http://www.homeofheroes.com/wings/part1/3b_cherami.html; http://www.homeofheroes.com/wings/part1/3_lostbattalion.html

13. "Pigeon Intelligence." Wikipedia. http://en.wikipedia.org/wiki/Pigeon_intelligence;
Urmee Kahn, 2008. "Pigeon's Intelligence Compared to a Three-Year-Old." Telegraph.co.uk. June 13, 2008. http://www.telegraph.co.uk/news/newstopics/howaboutthat/2125306/Pigeons-'intelligence'-compared-to-a-three-year-old-child.html#continue

14. Natalie Angier, 2008. "Noble Eagles, Nasty Pigeons, Biased humans." *The New York Times.* April 29, 2008. http://www.nytimes.com/2008/04/29/science/29angi.html

15. "The Plight of the Songbirds." Starry skies. http://starryskies.com/articles/dln/8-97/cowbirds.html
http://nationalzoo.si.edu/ConservationAndScience/MigratoryBirds/Fact_Sheets/default.cfm?fxsht=3;

16. "Cain and Abel." http://www.goodseed.com/cainandabel.aspx

17. Dennis Bratcher, 2006. "Old Testament Sacrifice: Magic or Sacrament?" July 19, 2006. http://www.cresourcei.org/sacrifice.html;
Wil Pounds, 2008. "Blood of Atonement." Abide in Christ: http://www.abideinchrist.com/messages/lev17v11.html

SEE ANIMALS THROUGH YOUR HEART!

Visit my websites and join me
as we unite worldwide to love and protect
our animal companions
and other critters of Nature.

www.MaggieWright.net
www.BringingBackTheMagic.com
www.NaturesCornerMagazine.com
www.AnimalLoversUnited.com
www.AfricanGreys.com
www.AfricaNature.com
www.WrightMarketingBlueprint.com